The Psalm 91 Project

...Heavenly Backup for Law Enforcement Officers.

by David Wlazlak

The Psalm 91 Project

…Heavenly Backup for Law Enforcement Officers

Copyright © 2010 by David P. Wlazlak

Revised Version (2) / Edition (2) 12/03/2022/ Paperback /

Minor Updates /About Author Page Updated 12/03/2022

KDP ISBN: 9798837018633

Created in the United States of America

All rights reserved by the author. No reprint permitted without expressed written permission from the author or author's designees(s). Author Contact: literaryprojectsdpw@gmail.com

All scripture quotations, unless otherwise indicated, are taken from the New King James Version®. Copyright © 1982 by Thomas Nelson, Inc. Used by permission. All rights reserved.

NIV reference on page 43 is from HOLY BIBLE, NEW INTERNATIONAL VERSION ® Copyright © 1973, 1978, 1984 by International Bible Society. Used by permission of Zondervan Publishing House. All rights reserved.

Disclaimer: The views expressed in this book or cover neither represent the views of the CBP or the United States nor are endorsed by them. 5 C.F.R. § 2635.807(b)(2).

Disclaimer: The author is not a psychologist or counselor and makes no claim to be one. If any person (including the reader) uses the information in this book based upon his or her constitutional rights and interpretations of the material, the author and/or publisher assume no responsibility for actions taken by any person.

CONTENTS

Preface 5

Acknowledgements 7

Dedication 8

Psalm 91 9

Promise One
Psalm 91:1 11

Promise Two
Psalm 91:2 15

Promise Three
Psalm 91:3 19

Promise Four
Psalm 91:4 23

Promise Five
Psalm 91:5 29

Promise Six
Psalm 91:6 37

Promise Seven
Psalm 91:7 43

Promise Eight
Psalm 91:8………………………………………….. 47

Promise Nine
Psalm 91:9…………………………………………... 51

Promise Ten
Psalm 91:10…………………………………………… 55

Promise Eleven
Psalm 91:11-12………………………………………. 59

Promise Twelve
Psalm 91:13……………………………………….. 65

Promise Thirteen
Psalm 91:14………………………………………….. 71

Promise Fourteen
Psalm 91:15……………………………………….. 75

Promise Fifteen
Psalm 91:16……………………………………….. 79

Unified Prayer of Protection for Law Officers…….. 85

About the Author……………………………………89

PREFACE

Without a doubt, there are excellent teachings available on Psalm 91. An internet search will provide plentiful study materials on this Messianic Psalm. I am appreciative of anyone willing to read what I have written regarding God's promise to the Christian church for divine protection. Even though this project encompasses a little more than twenty-two thousand words – it is only a gleaning of what is teachable from this life changing Psalm.

Of course, there is a limited amount of teaching about this subject for law enforcement officers (LEOs) who have signed up to protect and serve our towns, cities, states, and nations from criminals hard spent on bringing anarchy to pass.

This is why the Precious Holy Spirit compelled me to write these short essays on Psalm 91. It will absolutely help us LEOs to overcome the vast stresses we encounter in our service roles, as it puts fear in its proper place.

FEAR – its only positive contribution keeps us alert and aware of the dangers we face. However, we must ensure it does not paralyze us from responding appropriately and in faith.

I searched many venues to find teachings related to Psalm 91 that were specific for the law enforcement community. Unfortunately, I was unable to discover a compilation of essays on each verse explaining how they relate to law enforcement servanthood; hence, The Psalm 91 Project was born. You have before your eyes a line-by-line teaching on the most trusted Psalm of protection available to the Christian church. This book is specifically written to those who have made any arm of law enforcement their career. Above all, I am thankful the Holy Spirit allowed me to participate in this project.

I invite You to join me and other brothers and sisters in law enforcement on an insightful journey through this Psalm most likely written by Moses. It has the potential to do more for you than any class of defensive tactics, pursuit driving, or weapons proficiency that you have taken.

In Christ,

David Wlazlak

ACKNOWLEDGEMENTS

With gratitude and heartfelt recognition, I would like to thank KRISTIE WLAZLAK and SCOTT BRENKERT for their role in grammatical and content revisions.

Thank You!

DEDICATION

I dedicate this book to my mother MARY GRACE WLAZLAK, who crossed over to be with Jesus on October 27, 2005. The remembrance of her saying, "David, almost nothing worth doing is easy" assisted me in persevering through the completion of this project.

PSALM 91

Safety of Abiding in the Presence of God

He who dwells in the secret place of the Most High Shall abide under the shadow of the Almighty. 2 I will say of the Lord, "He is my refuge and my fortress; My God, in Him I will trust."

3 Surely He shall deliver you from the snare of the fowler And from the perilous pestilence. 4 He shall cover you with His feathers, And under His wings you shall take refuge; His truth shall be your shield and buckler. 5 You shall not be afraid of the terror by night, Nor of the arrow that flies by day, 6 Nor of the pestilence that walks in darkness, Nor of the destruction that lays waste at noonday.

7 A thousand may fall at your side, And ten thousand at your right hand; But it shall not come near you. 8 Only with your eyes shall you look, And see the reward of the wicked.

9 Because you have made the Lord, who is my refuge, Even the Most High, your dwelling place, 10 No evil shall befall you, Nor shall any plague come near your dwelling; 11 For He shall give His angels charge over you, To keep you in all your ways. 12 In their hands they shall bear you up, Lest you dash your foot against a stone. 13 You shall tread upon the lion and the cobra, The young lion and the serpent you shall trample underfoot.

14 "Because he has set his love upon Me, therefore I will deliver him; I will set him on high, because he has known My name. 15 He shall call upon Me, and I will answer him; I will be with him in trouble; I will deliver him and honor him. 16 With long life I will satisfy him, And show him My salvation." NKJV

PROMISE ONE

Psalm 91:1

He who dwells in the secret place of the Most High Shall abide under the shadow of the Almighty.

I **LOVE THE BIBLE!** It truly has everything we need within its pages to assist in fulfilling our obligations as law enforcement officers. Of course, the Word of God is applicable to all areas of our lives. Psalm 91 gives assurance that when things go haywire, we have supernatural backup in the spiritual realm. These tactical response units (Angels) are anticipating an opportunity to help us get the upper hand in bringing evildoers to justice.

Psalm 91 starts off by saying: He who dwells! That means God is allowing all who desire to partake in the blessings of His secret place to benefit from the promises of protection recorded in His infallible Word. Truly, this applies to LEOs who are in harms way. Some may ask, "What and where His Secret Place is?" It is in the heart where their relationship with God grows each day, releasing the benefits of protection promised in Psalm 91.

Many people believe they are unqualified to make a claim on the scriptures; this is just a lie birthed from religious traditions and the forces of evil that want us to believe our worth to God is infinitesimal (immeasurably small). Luckily, we know the value of something is determined by what someone is willing to pay for it – and John 3:16 says, "God so loved the world that He gave His only begotten Son, that whoever believes in Him should not perish but have everlasting life."

Since God has provided His Son as the means to reconcile all of humanity back to Him, which by the way includes you as well, how much does that make You worth to Him? PRICELESS!

What does it mean to abide under the shadow of the Almighty? Well, the answer really is quite exciting! Because we have entered into a personal relationship with God our Father, Jesus, and the Holy Spirit, we are considered as being 'In Christ'. This means, along with many other benefits that fear has been replaced with peace. I guess one could say we have taken up spiritual residence in heaven with Jesus while His Spirit simultaneously dwells within us. Some things we must take on faith because they just sound to good to be true. One such scripture makes this clear in the book of Colossians 1:26-28 where it states: "the mystery which has been hidden from ages and from generations, but now has been revealed to His saints. To them God willed to make known what are the riches of the glory of this mystery among the Gentiles: which is Christ in you, the hope of glory."

Although, refusing to apply the promises of God's Word disqualifies us from reaping their full benefits. It is similar to being beneficiaries of a will, but never exercising our right to the legal inheritance left to us. Likewise, the only foolproof way to make a claim within the spiritual realm is to speak up and make our presence known. This is one reason speaking Psalm 91 each day before we report to duty is so important.

Without a doubt, it is our responsibility to stay rooted in our rightful place 'In Christ'. We do this by staking our claim within the middle of the circle surrounded by the Holy Trinity. After all, they are holding hands in complete unity around us.

To illustrate, imagine for a moment that God, Jesus, and the Holy Spirit have made a circle of protection around you. Well, for believers who are applying God's promises of protection to their lives, Psalm 91 becomes part of them.

Now, with that type of protection nothing can get to believers without getting past the angels dispatched by the Holy Trinity. You see, fear has no sustenance if we understand our place within the Trinitarian circle. If we choose to attach ourselves to Christ rather than to fear – we will be making a claim upon the promises in Psalm 91:1. Unfortunately, if we allow what we hear and see to paralyze us from speaking God's promises – we will have stepped out from the protective circle and shadow of the Almighty, into the closet of our deepest childhood fears.

PRAYER

The Great Almighty,

As Jesus dwells at Your right side we know He is making intercession for LEOs. He is our Great High Priest who sympathizes with all our weaknesses; and for this reason, we stand in faith knowing the Holy Trinity is protecting and watching out for our best interests. Above all, we proclaim that You are the refuge and fortress that protects. Because we know You, Jesus, and the Holy Spirit, there is power available that strengthens us to overcome every struggle. Thank You!

> Luke 17:6
>
> So the Lord said, "If you have faith as a mustard seed, you can say to this mulberry tree, 'Be pulled up by the roots and be planted in the sea,' and it would obey you.

PROMISE TWO

Psalm 91:2

I will say of the Lord, "He is my refuge and my fortress; My God, in Him I will trust."

IT HAS BEEN SAID THAT MOST PEOPLE'S PROBLEMS start right under their nose. I know that was the case with me during my adolescent years. It seemed that no matter how hard I tried; I was unable to keep my mouth shut. As my father would continuously say,

"David, a little bit of knowledge is a dangerous thing."

Furthermore, God has provided us with our mouth and vocal cords. He has given free will to use them for good or bad. For example, we have all been around the cynical law officers who consider it their collateral duty to spew venomous words against all those who do not agree with them. Their distrust provides credence to the truth that what someone habitually speaks will create an environment that is a merciless mirror of their spiritual condition. In other words, what a person has within him or her will determine what comes to them.

Obviously, most of all wars and conflicts get their fuel from words that are spoken in failed diplomacy. Not only that, but I grieve for failed marriages that have ended in divorce because of harsh words spoken in bitterness.

Likewise, just as words shape our world and future in the natural realm, they also proclaim our rightful place in the spiritual realm. This is why our confession in Jesus Christ and His promised protection as law enforcement officers is important. The question is: what are you saying about God, your life, and the protection His Word wants to provide you? Are you saying God is your refuge and fortress? Are you quoting Psalm 27:5 "For in the time of trouble He shall hide me in His pavilion; In the secret place of His tabernacle He shall hide me; He shall set me high upon a rock."

If I told you a sanctuary exists which provides freedom from worry, adversity, and tribulation - would you want to know where it is? Well, there just happens to be such a place, and the ticket to get there can be prayed into existence by your profession that the Lord is your refuge and fortress.

Unfortunately, there is a thief that stands nearby who desires to steal your ticket, and his name is Fear. His archenemy is Faith and they have an antipathy towards one another. Fear brings pressure against us, but faith counterattacks with promises from God's Word.

Subsequently, we may hesitate to speak the promises written in the Word of God because there is little voice that says, "You're a fool if you trust in God." The very fact that those thoughts come to us, only proves that what we confess is indeed possible to happen in our lives.

When I think of God's refuge, I imagine an island where the glory of God abides. Angels protect this secret place by encamping around it. Their unity creates an impenetrable fortress. A protected place from all the dangers Satan wants to bring our way.

You know the traps he desires to set for us including car accidents, ambushes, and temptations to engage in immorality and other activities that chip away at the foundation of our integrity.

Said differently, a spiritual dynamic occurs when we confess that our confidence is set in God. It places us apart from all those who believe God is their problem and the cause of all worldly hardships. We are saying God is good and our trust is placed 'In Him' to protect us. In all practicality, our words are setting the record straight and putting the blame back on who it belongs – Satan, demons, and those they influence.

To this end, because we have confessed that our trust is in God and not in our intellect, training, retirement, and backup - He will surely keep His Word because He has obligated Himself to it.

PRAYER

Most High God,

We commit to spend more time in Your Holy presence beholding Your beauty each day. We know that when we are in trouble You are with us. We will continue to rejoice by praising You all the days of our lives and forever more.

As a result, times of turmoil and stress will affect us like water upon a duck's back. With that said, we are victorious in everything we put our hands to, and our efforts are blessed by You.

Thank You for hearing when we pray and allowing us to dwell in Your Secret Place.

> Hebrews 11:6
>
> But without faith it is impossible to please Him, for he who comes to God must believe that He is, and that He is a rewarder of those who diligently seek Him.

PROMISE THREE

Psalm 91:3

Surely He shall deliver you from the snare of the fowler and from the perilous pestilence.

WE HAVE ALL HEARD THE SAYING: if something sounds too good to be true, it probably is. Most of the time that saying stands up to its skeptics, but when it comes to applying Psalm 91:3 to our lives, God's promises are SURELY 100% true. If God said it, you could take it to the bank knowing His Word is worth more than its weight in gold, and it will not require an F.D.I.C. government bailout to remain intact. After all, is God like a man who has a reason to lie?

Of course not!

Did you know Jesus was tempted in every fashion just as we are? Well, He was! He overcame those trials through trusting in the promises found all through God's Word. Because of this, His victory qualified Him to help us overcome weaknesses. As the anonymous writer of 'The Epistle to the Hebrews' wrote in chapter 2:18: "For in that He Himself has suffered, being tempted, He is able to aid those who are tempted."

You see, Jesus was tempted in everyway because Satan offered Him the entire earth and all nations of the world without having to go to the cross. Someone who is in complete control of the earth can indulge in anything he or she pleases. Therefore even though Jesus was not specifically tempted in every fashion; he was indirectly tempted because if he would have done it Satan's way no worldly desire could have eluded Him.

Of course, who really knows how God would have reacted if Jesus had failed the test. Moreover, the snare the fowler set for Jesus was the temptation to transcend to His rightful throne by stepping outside the parameters of obedience rather than redeeming humanity through the ordeal of the crucifixion.

Are you glad Jesus did not accept the devil's offer, but attained His High Priestly position through obedience rather than committing perfidy against God, succumbing to bribery, and leaving an ignominious legacy? I sure am! This is important to understand because if Jesus had to make a claim upon the promises to reap their benefits and overcome temptations (snares) – why would we be exempt from doing the same? Answer: we are not!

Surely, He provided a way to avoid the traps strategically placed in our lives by Satan, demons, and the unrighteous souls under their disposal. Trusting in God's Word provides spiritual reassurance that we are capable of recognizing truth. It also clears out the fog of deception so we can see clearly into the spiritual realm, allow our conscience to lead us, and recognize ploys diabolical entities have placed in our paths.

Allow me to give a little bit of background about the fowler. In ancient biblical times, a fowler was a hunter who would set traps for birds. When he or she ensnared the prey, this hunter would kill it or use it to barter. Upon capture, the birds became the fowler's to do with as desired.

Ensnared by the fowler, the birds had believed a lie that what they saw was the only thing they would get. I heard a minister preach on this passage of Psalm 91 and he used the example of how quail spend a lot of time walking on the ground rather than seeing things from a higher viewpoint. He stated that when he was a young boy, he would ensnare quail by setting a trap. Secretly, he would hide in the bushes holding on to the string attached to the stick lifting the wooden box at a 90-degree angle.

When the quail entered under the box for the prize, he would pull the string, trapping the bird. His point was to stay off the ground and in the transcended secret place with God where you can see the fowler's plan of chicanery.

Another trap of the fowler, indicative in law enforcement work, is the step many LEOs take to end their marriage by believing their adulterous companion would make them happier than their current spouse. Moreover, some have treated God's blessing as a curse and realized too little – too late, that they were married to a diamond in the rough and failed to recognize him or her in their unpolished form. The agony of deceptive defeat, foretold by early 20th century Pentecostal fire and brimstone evangelists described the consequences of being flesh led, by the saying, "Sin will always take you farther than you wanted to go, and cost you more than you ever thought it would." This malady suffered out through the financial hardship of divorce, maintaining two households, and paying spousal support; all of which are evident in the LEO's checkbook register and payroll garnishments. Of course, many LEOs' spouses are hugely different from a sparkling gem. As a wise mentor of mine once said, "When God gives you a spouse, He gives you an assignment." Unfortunately, the hardened hearts created by law enforcement work sometime prevent LEOs from overcoming marital difficulties. If this is hitting close to home, realize God's grace is sufficient to forgive and set your current marriage on the right road of recovery.

Well, this is quite interesting from our perspective as law officers because it is literally saying that the fowler (who in our case are Satan, demons, and the unrighteous) have actually dug pits for us to fall into and have covered them with fig leaves and branches. Those sheathings could be a callous heart towards God's Word, our agency management, and/or those depending on us to serve and protect them – which most assuredly includes our immediate families. Without a doubt, one trap is idolatry, which in practical terms is giving preference to anything above God in our lives. Of course, we would be negligent if we did not acknowledge the physical traps set by wicked people who desire to kill us as we prevent their rebellion, and the fear we face daily when dealing with people who have communicable diseases. Let us not forget the danger that accompanies self-righteousness birthed by works based religions, which just happened to be symbolic of the perilous pestilence that came against Jesus.

An even more dangerous trap is the unwise use of our tongue. Since the tongue expresses what is in the heart of an individual, it either seals the person's eternal destiny with God or separates the unbeliever from Him for all eternity. See: Romans 10: 8-12.

Truly, the most dangerous trap that has eternal consequences which is set for all mankind regardless of race, economic status, nationality, and religion – is the rejection of Jesus Christ as one's Savior and Lord; which is referred to in many religious circles as the unpardonable sin that leads to the pit of eternal fire. The Fowler (Satan) has strategically placed at the bottom of this hole a row of spikes that will pierce through its prey, resulting in a painful life of bondage and an eternity of no hope.

Is it nice to have assurance that we are not like those who do not have hope? When the unpredictable temptations of law enforcement servanthood send tidal waves of discouragement and danger our way – we can be sure to find refuge under the branches of the tree of life – Who is Jesus the Christ!

PRAYER

God Who Delivers,

We proclaim: the demon forces that came against Jesus were completely defeated by Him, and we are victorious against all who come against us because of our relationship with You. Above all, we rebuke all sickness and disease. Thank You!

PROMISE FOUR

Psalm 91:4

He shall cover you with His feathers, and under His wings you shall take refuge; His truth shall be your shield and buckler.

IF I WERE TO TELL YOU that when people come against You they are actually messing with God – what would You say? Yeah right, would be most peoples' response. Many law enforcement officers, deceived by religious traditions, but who have humbled their pride and accepted Jesus as their personal Lord and Savior, would more than likely shrug at such a statement. Well, hold on to your hat because the powerful Holy Ghost wind is about to shake some of your religious foundations. Especially those built upon tradition rather than truth.

WHEN PEOPLE COME AGAINST YOU, THEY ARE MESSING WITH GOD; OF COURSE, THAT IS IF YOU ARE A BORN-AGAIN CHRISTIAN. My experiences and studies have contributed to a personal inference that God sometimes turns His back on those who persecute Christians. In a way, He seems to allow them to become victims of circumstance as they reap what they have sown. Rather than personally coming against them, God simply removes all protection from their life. Spiritually, the evil previously suppressed around them harasses the evildoer without fear of God's wrath. One biblical example of this is in the book of Acts. Herod the king, who was mercilessly persecuting Christians, had intended to execute Peter. The Church prayed and the Angel of the Lord rescued Peter. Shortly after, Herod was struck by the Angel of the Lord and was eaten of worms and died. I believe Herod always had had bacteria eating worms in his body; but when the Angel of the Lord struck him, he lost God's protection and it became replaced with an unrestricted feeding frenzy of microscopic biological worms that had been dormant in his body. Possibly, God will even gracefully protect the unbeliever up until the time he or she perniciously hinders the advancement of the gospel. I guess a finger-pointing legalist could conclude that when it goes down like this, God is walking the line of contributory manslaughter. See: Acts Chapter 12.

In the first place, the proof of salvation, that overwhelming state of nirvana brought to fruition through faith in Christ's resurrection from the dead, has taken ownership of the spirit-man through the impartation of Christ's Spirit. Released, like a bird that was caged, the believer is free to fly high and far away from the once accepted confine of life - that prison of condemnation. To illustrate, imagine a priceless, rare, and highly sought-after gold coin. One side represents the Godly authority LEOs derive their power from and the other is symbolic of the enlightenment that comes when one's spirit transcends his or her ego. While looking closely, one can see a circular pattern interconnected by the words faith, trust, hope, and love.

Within the circle is a picture of Jesus Christ holding a powerful representation of God's Word, that two-edged battle sword God uses to cut straight into the prideful attitudes of humankind. In Jesus' right hand is the defensive shield all Christians have within their arsenal, the ability to control their thoughts. Equally important, impressed within the metal of one side of the sword is an image of God's Heavenly dwelling place – The Holy of Holies. The other side inscribed from the base of the metal to the narrowing of the tip is the saying: The Word and the Spirit. In Jesus' right hand, embossed in a raised fashion across the shield is an image of two large mountains with a chasm between them. One range has the word deception chiseled into its foundation; the other has the word truth carved in its base. The gorge between them represents the lies that come from one's mind, will, and emotions; those foreboding feelings of low self-worth, the beliefs that hinder so many from accepting God's love, and acquiescing to the lie they are not valuable in His eyes.

This is the reason they stay separated from the peace found on God's rock of truth. Their disbelief in His greatness keeps them in the jurisdiction of deceptive despondency. Luckily for them there just happens to be a bridge connecting the two ranges together, but to have the right to use the overpass they have to pay the toll. Well, I have more good news because the fare requires them to exchange the plastic coin they inherited from their spiritual father (Satan) at natural birth, for the heavenly gold coin that represents reconciliation to God. The worldly inferior coin has self-generated pride written on one side and selfishness inscribed on the reverse. It has no intrinsic value and pollutes the earth. God knows that its chemical elements are a suitable fuel source to keep Hell burning. He requires all humankind to use it as payment to walk from the mountain range of deception, above the valley of low self-worth, into the arms of Jesus Christ.

The other side of the heavenly minted gold coin is engraved with two angels hovering above the born-again believer(s), as he or she rest peacefully in the assurance of God's presence. Their sense of knowing they are safe is because God is living within them, and inimitable heavenly angels protect anywhere His Spirit dwells.

To illustrate, during Old Testament times, the presence of God dwelled in a Holy Relic – the Ark of the Covenant. Now, He dwells in every person who has accepted His unmerited grace, the forgiveness of sins Jesus of Nazareth provided for all. That is correct, God is living in you, and the Holy Angles are protecting everything and everyone He inhabits, including your body. I am not asking you to only take my word for it; but read what the Apostle Paul wrote concerning this: Do you not know that you are the temple of God and that the Spirit of God dwells in you? If anyone defiles the temple of God, God will destroy him. For the temple of God is holy, which temple you are. 1 Corinthians 3:16-17

We can take this insight to a deeper understanding by applying it to the entire body of Christ – not just individual believers. Most definitely, no weapon formed against the church can prosper when she stands on the promises in the bible. God has promised in Psalm 91 that He will cover us with His feathers. Because of this truth, we are beneath His wings. Well, this is like the terminology that is in other passages of the Bible. For instance, even in the book of Exodus God is recorded as saying to Moses, "You have seen what I did to the Egyptians, and how I bore you on eagles' wings and brought you to Myself." Exodus 19:4

Sure, some may say the Israelites had an uncommon deliver to help them during the trials that ensued because of the slavery they were under; and that is a correct proclamation. After all, they did have Moses representing them, who went to Pharaoh and demanded that he let God's people go.

It is common knowledge to all who have seen the 1956 American motion picture called: 'The Ten Commandments', starring Charleston Heston, that God's will was manifested after Moses promulgated it to a hardhearted idolatrous Pharaoh after ten horrific plagues proved the Egyptian gods were no match for Jehovah. Now, ponder this question for a moment: If God protected the Israelites, who did not have the Holy Spirit dwelling within them, how much more will He fulfill promises of protection and deliverance towards born-again Christian law officers upholding His societal system of order, walking under the influence of His indwelling Spirit? Our uncommon deliverer is Jesus the Christ and He said, "In My Father's house are many mansions; if it were not so, I would have told you. I go to prepare a place for you. And if I go and prepare a place for you, I will come again and receive you to Myself; that where I am, there you may be also." John 14:2-3

Unlike what 21st century traditional theology teaches; the above passage does not give credence to the doctrine that Jesus is in heaven building us a literal house. Even though He was a carpenter by trade while on earth, He is not walking around heaven with a tool belt strapped around His waist and a hammer in His hand, carefully avoiding the pain associated with missing the nail's head and smashing His thumb. Of course, Jesus did go and prepare a place for us; but that occurred when He rose from the dead. That place is the abode He took up residence in when He returned. For us believers He has become one with our spirit-man who lives in our earth-suit (body). Therefore, we who are 'In Christ' are already resting in the refuge of the Holy Spirit: the place Jesus prepared in our heart after God resurrected Him from the dead. Those who accept and apply this truth can live under the protection of His wings, similar to the way a mother hen protects her chicks. The good news is that by placing our faith and trust in God, He protects us from the arrows of discouragement that are shot at our mind, while covering our back and side from unseen threats aimed at our blind sides. Simply said, "He is our shield and buckler." The Apostle Paul knew this truth and he reminded the Jerusalem saints that God said, "No man shall be able to stand before you all the days of your life; as I was with Moses, so I will be with you. I will not leave you nor forsake you." Joshua 1:7

I am not saying we should react heedlessly, without wisdom, by failing to implement the training necessary to protect others and ourselves; but I am standing on the firm foundation of truth that the Apostle Paul so adamantly proclaimed: For He Himself has said, "I will never leave you nor forsake you. So we may boldly say: "The Lord is my helper; I will not fear. What can man do to me?" Hebrews 13:5-6

PRAYER

God Who Covers Us with Your Wings,

With the promises in Your Word, along with our relationship with the Great High Priest Jesus and the Holy Spirit – we have no reason to fear. We give praise to Your Name for hearing when we pray and allowing entrance into the Holy of Holies to have fellowship with You. Thank You!

> Hebrews 11:29
>
> By faith they passed through the Red Sea as by dry land, whereas the Egyptians, attempting to do so, were drowned.

PROMISE FIVE

Psalm 91:5

You shall not be afraid of the terror by night, Nor of the arrow that flies by day.

WE WEAR OUR BODY ARMOR, train in defensive tactics, and maintain proficiency with both lethal and non-lethal service weapons.

Why?

Because surviving on the streets and in the prisons requires preparedness to respond tactically. The tools of our trade are many and diverse – they save the lives of thousands each year. We are told in Psalm 91:5 not to be afraid of the terror by night, nor of the arrow *(bullet of sorrow)* that flies by day. *(Emphasis mine)*.

Most assuredly, when our lives are in danger there is an expected amount of fear as our blood pressure increases and our adrenalin kicks in. These are good in the way they keep everything in perspective and contribute to a heightened sense of awareness. When bullets are whizzing past us, it is wise to have taken threats seriously by proactively confessing the 91st Psalm before we left home. After all, we can use all backup available, regardless if it arrives from the natural or the spiritual realm.

When a LEO is cut-down in the line of duty, it adversely affects the entire law enforcement community. There is outrage which fuels a relentless pursuit of bringing the perpetrator(s) to justice, and rightly so.

Usually what follows are reactive measures including additional training and procedural changes all with the hope of preventing disheartening outcomes from occurring again.

In the year 2000, we lost 150 LEOs in the line of duty at the hands of criminals. When I think about the agencies that had to ride the bereavement rollercoaster, along with the families and friends of those officers, my inner man grieves.

Without a doubt, the works of evil were behind the motivations and intentions of those who committed those atrocities against God's ministers of law enforcement. Don't be fooled or believe for one minute that Satan and his cohort only come against LEOs by convincing the rebellious to take them out. Satan is using a wise plan to remove those standing in his way; and has been doing it with little to no resistance for far too long.

If I were to inform you that Satan devised a plan that creates animosity between the ranks of every law enforcement agency in the world – would you want to know what it is?

What if this master plan of destruction included blaming everyone within the LEO community for the deaths of thousands of law officers rather than addressing the cognitive and spiritual ramifications that led to their funerals. Surely, your anger would increase above 212 degrees, producing the steam to move the locomotive of bureaucracy over the highest peak of insensitive autocratic leadership.

If I told you, he has been utilizing this plan since the first officer stepped into the role of upholding the societal system of order – would your curiosity increase?

Well, there is such a plan currently in motion and its objective to deceive LEOs to commit suicide is manifesting itself in record numbers. The name I call it is "LEO Soul Control" and it was responsible for the deaths of 418 of our brothers and sisters in arms during the year 2000 and hundreds more afterwards.

Allow me to give you a little bit of background. The word "soul" is derived from the Greek word "psuche," and it is used to delineate an individual's mind, will, and emotions. It is the root of our modern terms of "psyche" or "psychology." The New Testament clearly states that demonic entities are conducting warfare by attempting to impart untrue perceptions (strongholds) of what is or is not acceptable behavior on our part. Many of these paradigms develop from traditions, prejudices, and experiences. Because behavior ensues from our perspectives and perceptions, it is essential that we are telling ourselves the truth. The Devil is the father of lies and manipulates people and circumstances to charge up our emotional batteries. He does this because emotions work like biological chemicals sometimes creating illusions – much like hallucinatory drugs. We put up a defense against these attacks when we pray, meditate in God's Word, and practice fallibilism – accepting the possibility there is more to a situation than what our auditory and visionary systems are revealing.

As we continue down the road of law enforcement servanthood, we encounter disheartening incidents failing to stop and access our mental health. The rookie officer is most at risk of making this career-damaging mistake. He or she usually passes by the first rest stop because of the excitement and adrenalin rush of being in a reoccurring state of hyper-vigilance.

Moreover, the officer obliviously speeds past the educational pamphlets available that explain the biological symptoms law enforcement work can have on the body – such as a decline in doing activities that used to give him or her pleasure before they were an LEO, chemical imbalances in the brain, and the warning of becoming less autonomous each passing year.

A few miles down the road (or years in our case); this same officer witnessed some roadkill along the highway. Maybe he or she even had to maneuver past the dead carcasses in their path; like public complaints against them, critical incidents, and failed relationships with their significant others. The cost of not taking that first rest stop has allowed the experiences he or she has faced to weaken their resolve, not to mention the putrid smell from all those carcasses.

Out of necessity, the seasoned law officer exits 'Servanthood Highway' by pulling off at the next rest stop. Upon exiting his or her patrol vehicle, they see a sign that says, "Stop Here and Rest Awhile." Next to the sign is a picnic table that has messages embedded in the wood. Some of them say, "Look at all you have given to society and for what? Before you took this job you thought you would be making a significant difference in your community – what a lie – it has stripped you of the freedom you previously had over your life."

Another line says, "Your department has violated its trust towards you; therefore, the rules they want you to follow no longer apply – it is only right for you to be able to get your fair share." The picnic table is covered with carvings that play upon the thought patterns of the law officer as he or she sits there reading one after another. The more the officer reads those destructive sayings the more likely he or she is to believe them. Too bad, they do not know that vindictive little demons sit at the table every night carving those half-baked truths into its wood. After planted seeds of discontent and unfairness find a home in the mind of the officer, he or she proceeds back to the vehicle. Upon opening the door, the officer notices a rip in the seat of his or her older model Crown Vic. Immediately; the LEO remembers how the officer right out of the academy is assigned a newer model with more features than his or her cruiser. Out of the officer's mouth proceeds the seeds of discontent by saying, "This attests to the fact that everything I just read on that picnic table is true, there must be a better way to get what I deserve."

The words of negativity they speak are like arrows that fly towards others with the intentions of causing the premature demise of their positive attitude. When around the cynical officer and others who profess calumnies we need to protect us and them by praying Psalm 31:20 that says, "You shall hide them *(us)* in the secret place of Your presence from the plots of man; You shall keep them *(us)* secretly in a pavilion from the strife of tongues." *(Emphasis mine)*.

Thereafter, as the officer begins towards 'Servanthood Highway' leading to the City of Purpose, he or she sees the frontage road to their right. Since 'Servanthood Highway' has not yielded the officer the carnal fruits he or she thought it would, they decide to take a different route.

Unfortunately, the name of that frontage road is Servitude and it leads to the cities of Self-Interest, Fear, and Slavery. Within the first few miles traveling upon that route the officer becomes more cynical towards everyone he or she does not agree with, and manifests that distrust by trying to run over any agency manager they feel uncomfortable around – who in most cases is everyone that holds a position of authority over them.

The officer's animosity is the result of the behavior mechanisms he or she has been leaning on to overcome the danger felt around those who control his or her career. Even worse than not having control over his or her law enforcement assignment is the lack of autonomy in their personal life because of rotating shift work and/or excessive overtime. This contributes to over investing in their LEO role. As statistics prove, too many LEOs have succumbed to the danger of excessive interconnectedness in their police-roles, manifested in their inability to differentiate between themselves and the badge they wear.

Since they cannot attack their agency administrators physically, they come up with a different plan of sabotage. It starts by sowing seeds of discontent against management among other officers. They do not stop there by any means and begin to file grievances, and if the perfect storm of negative circumstances come barreling down on them they lose all hope, and in their mind attempt to settle the score by freeing themselves from their emotional pain through suicide. Their twisted reasoning that led to that irrevocable decision of self-interest was likely the culmination of build-up stress, deception, and depression. Of course, there is always the possibility that it was a physiological disorder ensued by psychological manifestations. In most cases, the act that removed them from reaching the destination they initially set out for may have been preventable with the proper emotional survival training and spiritual weaponry. It is an interesting conundrum why law enforcement agencies invest thousands of dollars training officers how to survive on the streets but fail to recognize the necessity of equipping them with knowledge to remain psychologically healthy.

Yep, that is a mouthful for sure, and many police psychologists have made their livelihood treating the symptoms law enforcement work has upon the psyche of LEOs. Unfortunately, many of them have concentrated too much on the important biological feedback and psychological causes, while disregarding the spiritual roots to the problem.

Since humans are three-part beings (body, soul, and spirit) the solutions must address each part in proportion to the root causes that suck the life out of the officer. If we ask the Lord to solve this problem for us as he did for the writer of Psalm 116:3-4, our souls will be delivered from the wiles (tricks and schemes) of Satan and/ or his cohorts.

> Psalm 116: 3-4
>
> The pains of death surrounded me, and the pangs of Sheol laid hold of me; I found trouble and sorrow. Then I called upon the name of the Lord: "*O Lord, I implore You, deliver my soul!*" *(Emphasis mine).*

To this end, can you see how Psalm 91:5 and other promises in God's Word address and solve the problems we face in our law enforcement roles? It gives hope that if we control what we think about, ensure we are telling ourselves the truth, and maintain our attitude of service through purpose – we will be lifting up the shield and buckler (verse 4) which will protect us from the terror of servitude and its surmising objective; which is to get us to disqualify ourselves from making any meaningful change in the world.

PRAYER

God Who Delivers Us from Sorrow,

Oh Lord, we need Your help in a grand way. Law enforcement officers are committing suicide at alarming rates; however, it seems that too few are responding to the call of this epidemic. Please move upon the management and leadership of every law enforcement agency on earth to implement suicide prevention and emotional survival training to their officers.

As You know Lord, law enforcement officers are committing suicide at two times the rate of line of duty deaths. This should grieve the hearts of those that have authority in their agencies to make significant changes that benefit their officers. It saddens us when they continue to treat officers worse than cattle by being completely insensitive to their needs, and the ramifications hyper-vigilance has on their personal and professional lives. We are grateful because You hear and respond when we pray. Thank You!

> Hebrews 11:1
>
> Now faith is the substance of things hoped for, the evidence of things not seen.

PROMISE SIX

Psalm 91:6

Nor of the pestilence that walks in darkness, Nor of the destruction that lays waste at noonday.

AS THE GLORIOUS LIGHT OF JESUS CHRIST SHINES upon the cultures, governments, and religious establishments of any given era – the pestilence that walk's in darkness lays dormant in the cursed earth. No angel, fallen or obedient to God is unaware that disease, sickness, and poverty cannot flourish epidemically when the glorified benefits of faith in God's Word are taught, imparted, and applied to the lives of Christians. You may be asking, "What exactly are you saying Brother David?"

Well, this is how I see it. During the 1340's, there was a plague that was caused by fleas that had hitched rides on the backs of the rodents throughout Europe. These nasty little bacteria carrying Xenopsylla cheopis (Rat flees) were the cause of the notorious Bubonic Plague - a life sucking, blood infecting pestilence. The plague received credit for killing almost 20 million people in that region of the world and more than 1000 a day in the City of Tunis, North Africa. Many historians and scholars have referred to that time span as the Dark Ages; although the exact dates for the term are, debated, spiritual darkness was hovering over that region of the world preventing the glorious light of the gospel message from being promulgated. In our current age of inordinate sensitivity that has given birth to excessive political correctness, and the enlightened view that every period of time has contributed positively to the benefits of human exploration, the term that was once given to that era is often referred to now by some scholars as: The Middle Ages.

Regardless of the term we use to describe this period, one truth will always remain and it is simply this: the diaphanous light of Jesus Christ's healing message, the preserving spiritual salt that would have prevented the Black Plague of that era from exercising a reign of disease upon the populace, was being suppressed by an Anti-Christian Religion. What ensued was ignorance of Satan's devices on a grand scale that manifested in the natural realm through deadly pestilence. It is essential to know that the prophet Isaiah and Apostle Peter wrote that Jesus took all our infirmities and healed all of our diseases. Without this insight, divine health may elude us. See: Isaiah Chapter 54 & 1 Peter 2:24.

Even though science has made extraordinary leaps since the Middle Ages there are still hot agents (killer viruses) residing in dark and murky places, patiently waiting for suitable hosts to attach themselves. Once inside the victim they take passage through the blood, feeding off the organs as a frontal and rear assault simultaneously supplants territory the white blood cells once ruled. These pernicious microorganisms devour from within causing internal bleeding as the blood searches for away of escape through every orifice of the body. As the victim grows weaker, the virus grows stronger with an unquenchable appetite to infect its next victim: the hapless first responder - possibly a brother or sister LEO. These filo-viruses have been manifesting unexpectedly throughout the ages, alluding scientists and mocking illustrious researchers who proclaim these diseases have been around from the formation of the earth as they continue to overcome all odds, survive through dormant periods of human non-existence, and emerge violating the rules of practical science by jumping across species; these sister criminals of the bio-world are known and feared across the globe, they are one reason for biohazard space suits, they are agents of bio-warfare, and they are loathed in military Level 4 laboratory installations, their names are: Marburg and Ebola. However, we do not have to fear them!

When we allow Jesus Christ and His Word to have priority in our lives, our obedience to Him will produce unprecedented amounts of power which will overcomes all sickness and disease.

I have never seen Jesus; however, if I were a gambling man, I would bet my entire 401k that the light, which glows from Him, is so diaphanous that absolutely nothing diabolical can stand in His presence – including hot agents. Part of the good news reassures that His light lives and shines within us the brightest when we give Him priority by standing on God's promises. I agree with the respected bible teacher, author, and leader Joyce Meyer who stated, "Making God first is the key to experiencing His best."

I will make the inference that one of Jesus' intentions for saying, "I am the light of the world. He who follows Me shall not walk in darkness but have the light of life" was to help us understand that when we are walking 'In Him', the spiritual dangers lurking in the darkness cannot hurt us. These include the pestilence referred to in Psalm 91: 6 and any other sickness or disease

Our responsibility is to feast on God's Word preventing demonic entities carrying deadly pestilence from exiting the darkness. Our spiritual vigilance, like speaking scriptures of divine healing, will curtail the opportunities for disease having an opportunity to make a leap of faith toward us. The directions to stay on the lighted path are in the bible – they keep us safe through the jungle of sin all around us. See: John 8:12.

I would love to know exactly what Moses was thinking when he wrote Psalm 91. I am confident that as he and the Israelites were living in the wilderness there were many dangers of great concern to them such as venomous snakes, poisonous insects, and dangerous tribesmen, just to name a few.

I often wonder how many times during their forty years of wandering in the desert they were tempted to allow fear of unpredictable factors to control them, rather than the assurance they received from the cloud by day and the fire that led them by night. As we take God at His Word, we can enter the peaceful knowing that He will keep us safe.

> **Nor of the destruction that lays waste at noonday.**

September 11, 2001 will be remembered as the day the demon of diabolical destruction received his doctorate degree in wickedness. This noonday devil pulled off his most prestigious accomplishment of his miscreant career that morning, and he did it ahead of his noontime schedule. We witnessed the terror and horror that morning as self-righteous, suicidal religious fanatics, under the assumption they were doing the will of God, mercilessly murdered 2976 people. These homicidal maniacs hijacked and slammed two commercial jetliners into the Twin Towers in New York City, one into the Pentagon, and caused the terrifying decent of the fourth in a field near Shanksville, Pennsylvania. Those who fell that day included many of our LEO brothers and sisters who responded to render aid and safety to the victims. We will never forget them! The words spoken by Jesus echoed in my ears that morning as I recalled His prophetic utterance in John 16:2-3: "These things I have spoken to you, that you should not be made to stumble. They will put you out of the synagogues; yes, the time is coming that whoever kills you will think that he offers God service. In addition, these things they will do to you because they have not known the Father nor Me. But these things I have told you, that when the time comes, you may remember that I told you of them. John 16:1-4

Based upon that scripture one could confidently conclude that the god those terrorists were serving is not the same Deity Jesus knows. You may be asking, "Why didn't God prevent the horrible 9.11 atrocity from occurring?" or "Why didn't God protect the fallen that morning?" I agree these are legitimate questions and require some serious explanations.

Surely, there must have been Christians that died on 9.11 who trusted God to protect them. Maybe some of them new Psalm 91. So, what is the answer to these perplexing questions? Even more so, why do some law officers escape death at the hands of criminals and others do not?

The answers are in the universal law of free will. Being able to discern the voice of God and go around the dangers concocted in the depths of hell. You see, God has given each person on this planet the option to choose good or evil, to listen to his warnings, or reject them. Unfortunately, there are times people confuse what is good and what is evil and change the meanings to bolster their own preconceived prejudices. The bottom line is simply this: The problem with free will is people sometimes do things we do not want them to. **If we fail to pray and recognize our need for angelic intervention, we may become victims of their enormity.**

Our responsibility is to protect one another and ourselves. We do this by applying the Word of God to our life, listening to the Holy Spirit's warnings, being wise and cautious, and proactive praying. We may not be able to stop terrorists and criminals from the demonic patterns of thinking within their minds; but we can be sensitive to the Holy Spirit's warnings of danger ahead. Sometimes we just fail to recognize God's still voice when He warns of imminent danger in our path. I will say this: no one, including myself, is qualified to judge why many committed Christian LEOs have died in the line of duty – to do so would not only be judging their spirituality, but the faithfulness of God's Word. We just do not have all the information to know why the righteous are sometimes prematurely overtaken by evil.

What do we know?

We know Psalm 91 assures that God's protection is available. Even though we do not have the answers to many of our questions, we still have the option to choose good over evil by deciding to believe God rather than walk in fear. I will contend to concentrate on my responsibility regarding the promises of protection within this Psalm, rather than half-baked conjectures derived from religious platitudes – I invite you to join me by doing the same.

PRAYER

God Who Removed Fear,

We guard our peace by prohibiting Satan and His cohorts from stealing it. You have provided hope that passes all understanding and we refuse to doubt Your goodness. Assist in controlling our minds, wills, and emotions – for we know Satan comes against us through our thinking to paralyze with fear.

Moreover, he shoots false perceptions our way trying to convince that Your Word cannot protect from sickness and disease. Because of this we wear, our spiritual prayer vest to stop lies he shoots that are capable of causing internal injuries to our faith.

PROMISE SEVEN

Psalm 91:7

A thousand may fall at your side, And ten thousand at your right hand; But it shall not come near you.

SOME COMMENTARIES SAY JESUS WAS HANGING on the cross for nine hours. Just imagine nine hours of the worst form of torture known to humankind – crucifixion – reserved solely for the most heinous of criminals. Jesus waited for the exact moment in time for God's Wrath to fall upon the earth so He could willfully surrender His Spirit, knowing God would resurrect Him from the dead. I agree with the Apostle Paul who wrote, "You see, at just the right time, when we were still powerless, Christ died for the ungodly." Romans 5:6 NIV

Glory to God! Jesus fulfilled the predestined plan of reconciliation towards humanity. His obedience created the needed mercy to cancel out the wrath of God that had fallen upon the earth. Instead of judgment landing upon those who deserved it (all of humanity) – it settled upon Jesus' body in our stead.

The natural perception was Jesus had fallen short of God's assignment for His life, but that was not the reality. As we know, immediately after the crucifixion the disciples were overwhelmed with despondency.

Most likely, the wind beneath their wings had moved on towards the religious and political establishments of the day. Is it nice to know that even though Jesus' body was Spiritless, He was only temporarily out of the office taking care of some unfinished business in the afterlife?

Know this: everyone who died before the resurrection of Jesus Christ tasted the sting of death, which is separation from God; however, Jesus never tasted the sting of death like the one they had because Jesus and God were, and continue to be, interconnected in Spirit. As Jesus was walking through Paradise (Abraham's Bosom) and the depths of Hell, He clearly saw thousands that had experienced a hopeless death. These individuals, along with many fallen angels and other demonic entities, are some of those mentioned in Psalm 91:7.

Since we are 'In Christ' and were made 'In Him' we have overcome death's sting. With this knowledge, we understand that all those who do not know Jesus as their Savior will be eternally separated from God. Therefore, those who are lost in their sin and without Hope (Jesus) are unable to ward off spiritual death. These people are all around us, at our places of employment, jails, and places of worship.

Luckily, we have The Rod (The Word of God) to beat off the Demonic Death Angel when this entity comes for our soul and spirit; but those who are still living in darkness will not even see him coming. Once he grabs them, it will be too late to break free from his grip.

Eternity! Wow, we will live forever in a glorified body alongside Jesus and fellow believers. This is worth celebrating over – do you agree? It is reassuring to know that the promises in Psalm 91 do not only apply to future events such as the battle of Armageddon and the incarceration of Satan in the Lake of Fire. For example, the bible records many that came to earth before Jesus, who were justified by faith, and received divine assistance during perilous times. Noah could most assuredly testify of the tens of thousands who fell at his side as the flood waters raised above the pinnacles on the earth as he floated above them. Moreover, Abraham, the inexperienced warrior and father of the faith, under divine power annihilated thousands in the Battle of Dan. See: Genesis Chapter 14.

Even more astounding was how God delivered righteous Lot and his daughters from the fire and brimstone judgment that fell upon the cities of Sodom and Gomorrah. God did not stop protecting Abraham's decedents after that horrific event, but even showed His faithfulness by intervening repeatedly. The enslaved Hebrews stood by watching as the ten plagues came upon their Egyptian captors as they were residing safely in 'The Land of Goshen,' which means 'The Land of Drawing Near'. Similarly, we need to be drawing closer to God each day as the plagues of our current age come upon the earth – H1N1 Bird Flu, oil spills, global economic meltdown, tsunamis, terrorism, HIV, moral depravity etc.

Thereafter, while from front row seats, the Hebrews witnessed the Grand Finale of Pharaoh's army drowned in the Sea that God had previously parted for them. Now, if all that was not amazing enough, Jehovah out did Himself again with Gideon and three hundred of his men by defeating an army of 135,000 Midianite soldiers. I guess it would be safe to say that the draft was not needed to secure victory in Gideon's army. See: Judges Chapter 7

For sure, God proved the veracity of this Psalm long before it was ever written. We could say this Psalm is not only prophetic – meaning it truthfully foretold of the Messiah to come; but also historical in the way God had proven His faithfulness to the Hebrew people.

These facts are important for law officers to know and understand because they testify of God's willingness to help in our time of need. If by unfortunate chance the very nature of our assignment places us in a life or death situation that requires divine assistance in order to come up on top, we can make claim upon Psalm 91:7. When we mix our faith and confidence with it, we can rest assured that God will provide a helping hand. He did it for the great cloud of witnesses who are cheering for us as they observe from heavens grandstands and will render the same protection to us.

PRAYER

God Who Removed Fear,

Just as You protected the baby Jesus from the murderous agenda of king Herod, we know that when we are outnumbered and about to be defeated in battle, You will warn, protect, and lead us to victory. Likewise, as multitudes of police officers become suicidal statistics, our relationship with You will ensure we will not be one of them.

Thank You for hearing when we pray and giving us courage to trust You.

PROMISE EIGHT

Psalm 91:8

Only with your eyes shall you look, and see the reward of the wicked.

REBELLION IS ALL AROUND US, and if it were not for our commitment to keep it in check, anarchy would ensue upon our homeland contributing to its demise. In order to counteract evil, we must maintain vigilant, and move forward in eradicating criminality among the masses. Our task becomes difficult at times, especially when lying vanities holler the cliché, "crime really does pay," as it echoes throughout the auditory and vestibular pathways of our inner ears. Well, the Bible makes it clear that we will witness the recompense of evildoers for the selfishness they rendered towards their victims.

Moreover, there is a universal law that has been written in some form or fashion in every language known to humankind throughout the last 10,000 years. It encompasses both the natural and spiritual realms; and is taught in both secular and religious settings all over this blue planet that spins around the sun at speeds exceeding one thousand miles an hour. This law has not changed from the beginning of creation and has no favorites. Your curiosity has led you to ask, "What is the truth that has shaped the lives of thousands and has stood the test of time?" The answer is: The Law of Sowing and Reaping.

Maybe you have heard it defined as what a man sows he will surely reap or the more modern phrases: "You made your bed so lay on it" or "If you can't do the time, don't do the crime."

For sure these are accurate allegories portraying the reality occurring, as people are accountable for their actions, whether good or bad.

Now, something that will overtake the poisonous seeds we have planted is God's heavenly seed. To state, however, we will have to make the decision to allow it to work on our behalf and overtake the sin in our lives – that seed is faith. Faith seeds genetically contain DNA that provides reconciliation for all humanity to God. Many of the wicked refuse this priceless and free seed. These gospel rejecters willfully remain in their iniquitous condition failing to walk through the innocuous open door of Christ's flesh. It is sad they choose hell and death rather than heaven and eternal life.

Be encouraged in knowing this: not one criminal who fails to repent will be able to find a loophole that will allow him or her to be found not guilty in God's courtroom. Even if the natural system of law and order fails those it represents, God's jurisprudence will not be mocked. For sure, what they have sown they shall surely reap.

With these insights, we can continue in watchfulness without becoming discouraged and throwing in the towel. When danger confronts from any angle, we will witness the demise of the offenders and stand as a living testimony of Psalm 91:8.

As far as becoming discouraged because some of those we handcuff circumvent justice, we still have peaceful assurance that the weights and measurements will eventually reveal the truth. Unlike worldly justice systems, God's apothecary scale will not be fooled by the chicanery of any miscreants.

Regardless of the natural results of our efforts, we must maintain our presence in our towns, cities, states, and nations. The alternative is not acceptable and detrimental to ensuring people are protected from evildoers.

Know this: the righteous of God will witness the recompense of those who insisted on remaining unrighteous. After the Great White Throne Judgment foretold in Revelation 20, the wicked will be incarcerated for all eternity in the Lake of Fire. This truth is found in many biblical scriptures and was explained in detail by the Prophet Isaiah when he wrote: "For as the new heavens and the new earth which I will make shall remain before Me," says the Lord, "So shall your descendants and your name remain. And it shall come to pass That from one New Moon to another, And from one Sabbath to another, All flesh shall come to worship before Me," says the Lord. "And they shall go forth and look upon the corpses of the men who have transgressed against Me. For their worm does not die, and their fire is not quenched. They shall be abhorrence to all flesh" Isaiah 66:22-24

Well, there you have it – the promises in Psalm 91 have been, are currently, and will be fulfilled. It completely covers every generation that inhabited the four corners of planet earth. Just think about this for a moment: we will live on this renovated marble with Jesus for all eternity observing the wicked as they receive their reward – incarceration in the universal prison called: The Lake of Fire. With that said, next time we become discouraged over the uncontrollable injustices of law enforcement servanthood, we should realize that our LEO assignments assist in bringing offenders to a state of spiritual reflection. Possibly, our intervention may convince them to change their rebellious ways before they end up in the tormenting pit Isaiah described.

PRAYER

The Lord Who is Our Refuge,

We are thankful for all the Holy Spirit has and continues to do for us. He has made it perfectly clear in Psalm 91 that we will not suffer the consequences of the wicked.

Continually remind us that we are victorious when contending against anarchy. Above all, our conquering spirit will assist in bringing to pass the fruits of their unrighteous folly. Remind us that when it appears evildoers are prospering – we know they will eventually reap what they have sown. Thank You!

PROMISE NINE

Psalm 91:9

Because you have made the Lord, who is my refuge, Even the Most High, your dwelling place.

SOMETIME AGO, MAYBE ABOUT FIVE YEARS OR SO, I entered into a partnership with a local church where the Holy Spirit flows. It was obvious God called me there to provide various types of support, and in return, I would receive training to fulfill my ministerial calling. I highly recommend the hands-on impartation of the Word of God rather than correspondence and internet distance learning. Of course, one caveat to my belief system concerning this is being obedient to the Holy Spirit's leading.

As a respected mentor of mine says, "Some things are caught rather than taught." Just recently, I checked the file in my email account where I archive all my Pastor's correspondences and counted over three-hundred saved messages. Many recorded simple details regarding daily ministerial activities, advice, clarification, and a few warnings about wolves in sheep clothing. Without a doubt, I have grown in friendship through the years with him. These years of partnership have positively influenced the ministry and provided adequate prayer covering over my life.

You may be asking, "Why all this to start off a teaching on Psalm 91:9 or how does this even relate to this Great Psalm of Protection? The answer lies in one word. It is a word that determines who receives favor, protection, and support.... and who gets a kick in the.... you know what. Would you like to know what that word is? Well, here you have it. The magic word is RELATIONSHIP.

You see, to sail into your long sought-after destination, you must first realize that a ship is necessary to carry you to your harbor of growth. The vessel you jump aboard will have to have a captain who was trained in spiritual navigation while he or she was on the scout boat called Leadership. For you to reach your next port of call, you will have to hop aboard that captain's boat called Relationship. It is upon this boat you will have to set your sail and take advantage of the Holy Ghost wind. Most importantly, let us hope you do not miss the boat!

We have already inferred that Psalm 91 was written by Moses while he was inspired by the Holy Spirit. It was prepared by Moses to comfort the Messiah (Jesus) in His most trialing ordeal. As we are aware, Jesus had to depend on God to protect and raise Him from the dead. It is a logical conclusion based upon commonsense and an over-abundance of scripture that God, Jesus, and the Holy Spirit have a fortified relationship.

Jesus depended on this relationship to aid Him in remaining obedient to God's will. The Messiah knew this Psalm well. I have a picture in my mind of Him reading a large scroll and coming across this passage. I am convinced He realized that Moses wrote this Psalm for Him under the inspiration of the Holy Spirit. As Jesus studied it, He became more aware of the necessity to continue guarding His relationship with the Most High. Doing this would assure Him a place of protection and refuge. When Moses wrote, "Because You have made the Lord..." – he was referring to Jesus. The Holy Ghost speaking through Moses then said, "God is my refuge, He is the Most High, and that is where You (Jesus) dwell." The Holy Ghost's Refuge is God and Jesus dwells there with them.

Jesus is the subject of this passage of scripture and was aware of it. In my estimation, this is why He was able to go forward in confidence knowing that no evil would befall Him or any plague would come near His dwelling. Jesus overcame all evil and His dwelling (body) overcame the plague of death when He rose from the dead.

You see, the moment we enter into a personal relationship with Jesus Christ the darkness in our lives will be overtaken by light, and the benefits of divine protection will be within our grasp for the taking…just as it was available to Jesus. All of those not lucky enough to escape physical death through the rapture will indeed experience an out of body crossover into the spiritual realm. However, if they are born-again Christians a reuniting of their spirit will take place in the future with their resurrected body. Jesus did this first and showed what was to come for all those who know Him.

Since we are 'In Christ' and He has fulfilled all of God's requirements for us to be reconciled to Him, it is only logical to conclude that the protection promised in this psalm actually carries more weight for us than it did for Jesus.

Wow, now that will shake the very gates of Hell!

How is that you may be asking? The answer really is quite encouraging…it is simply this: The relationship between God, Jesus, and the Holy Spirit was strengthened as a result of Jesus' obedience to God's will and the increased trust they established among each other. Now, we are part of that relationship. Subsequently, we have the right to make claims upon it.

Our protection will be in direct proportion to the obedience we render towards Jesus, and the relationship we have with Him. Know this: the more we go through together…. the stronger our bond will be. This is one reason we have confidence as we wear our LEO uniform and report to duty. Our purpose is an extension of what Jesus came to accomplish, which just happens to be destroying the works of Satan as explained in 1 John 3:8-9, "He who sins is of the devil, for the devil has sinned from the beginning. For this purpose the Son of God was manifested, that He might destroy the works of the devil."

PRAYER

God Who Desires a Relationship with Us,

We desire to grow into a personal relationship with You, Jesus, and the Holy Spirit. It is through this type of intimacy that surrounds us by Your grace and protection. Furthermore, help us recognize any areas of our lives that are hindering our friendship with You. Assist us in tapping into the power available to overcome all idols.

PROMISE TEN

Psalm 91: 10

No evil shall befall you, Nor shall any plague come near your dwelling.

NO EVIL SHALL BEFALL YOU! Alternatively, in more modern-day language…no evil will happen to you! If I could purchase an insurance policy that had a promise such as this within its contract, I would say the words that I longed to hear when I was a used car salesmen: I will take it….write it up!

The Holy Spirit made quite a claim when He told Moses to write this verse. I am confident that any governmental regulating agency would be all over the above statement like flies on cow pies, as they probed into the insurance company making such claims to their customers. Let us be truthful with ourselves and admit that most Christians do not take this promise at face value. What comes to mind when I read Psalm 91: 10 is that most-encouraging promise in Ephesians 3:20 that states: Now to Him who is able to do exceedingly abundantly above all that we ask or think, according to the power that works in us.

Of course, that power is nothing less than the spiritual dynamite that raised Jesus from the dead. I believe it is safe to say that it carries enough protecting grace within it to keep us safe. Now, let us not forget that the initial beneficiary of this Psalm was Jesus of Nazareth, who was bestowed the Name above all names: Jesus the Christ. With this knowledge, we can do some serious analysis by asking the question, "Did anything bad happen to Jesus?" Ponder this: our Messiah was not the least bit affected by those who encountered Him that had medically incurable leprosy.

On another occasion, when He encountered the man with a legion of demons, the evil controlling that lost soul was so afraid of Jesus they pleaded with Him for mercy, requesting to inhabit a herd of pigs. If Jesus had denied their request, the county jail of wicked entities may have been their next destination. Would you agree with me that Jesus was not afraid of or affected in any way by the possibility of catching the swine flu?

Not one individual was able to lay a hand on Jesus until He allowed them. For sure, their intentions, even though deceptively evil, unknowingly participated in God's plan of reconciliation of humanity. We should not stop here, but during the storm on the Sea of Galilee He was never in danger. With all this said, I stand firm in my belief that no evil happened to Jesus while He was on earth and when He visited the fallen entities in Hell.

I would be wrong in saying that as LEOs we can walk around believing nothing can physically harm us. That is not faith, but foolishness. If you wear a ballistic vest, it may save you a premature demise. There are most definitely dangers we face. After all, we stand against the outward manifestations of the worst forms of evil. So, how does this portion of Psalm 91 apply to God's ministers of law enforcement? I am confident if you mused over it as I have you would come to the following inference: it indeed gives some sense of peace in knowing we have heavenly backup available. Because of this, we do not have to fear anything or anybody. The Holy Spirit and God's angels are there to help us overcome all threats biological, mental, physical, and spiritual.

For example, we are all aware of the stresses law enforcement servanthood produces. None of us is exempt from having to deal with cynicism, frustration, and temptations to partake in impropriety – using our trusted position for personal gain.

The thoughts of stepping outside our scope of employment under the lie that the end justifies the means sometimes creep in through the doors that open up into the cognitive rooms of our brain.

Within those chambers are the decisions leading to career successes or the agonies of defeat. Moreover, even though Jesus had every right to lash back in vengeance towards those who caused and carried out the crucifixion, He did not allow evil to overtake Him by allowing it to dictate a response contrary to holiness. If anyone had a right to lash out and demand His rights, or step spiritually backwards by not practicing self-control, it was Jesus of Nazareth.

Remember Peter, the man who denied Jesus three times but later repented and became a pillar of the church. He wrote about the way Jesus responded towards those who misjudged Him. Peter said, "For to this you were called, because Christ also suffered for us, leaving us an example, that you should follow His steps: "Who committed no sin, Nor was deceit found in His mouth"; who, when He was reviled, did not revile in return; when He suffered, He did not threaten, but committed Himself to Him who judges righteously; who Himself bore our sins in His own body on the tree, that we, having died to sins, might live for righteousness" (Peter 2:21-24)

You see, Jesus did not allow the circumstances of His trial to dictate His behavior. This example carries much weight because even if we perceive that we are victims of our agencies, fellow LEOs, or even those we are called to serve and protect….the decisions we make concerning our personal lives should still be based on God's Word, rather than the lie that if we compromise our integrity it doesn't matter.

We do not have a free pass to act out in unbecoming ways because of what we have experienced, seen, or come to believe concerning our victimization. Listen! It does matter what we do. If we allow evil to overtake the decisions we make in our professional and personal lives, we will have to deal with the plagues that ensue. Regardless, if they are secret idolatrous sins such as sex and internet porn that steal intimate time with God or the more stinky outward ones such as alcoholism, substance abuse, and gambling that purloin physical, spiritual, and financial health from LEOs.

For me, as a LEO and Christian minister, I am living in the secret place of the Most High: The Nation of Grace. I became a citizen of that Country through accepting Jesus Christ as my Lord and Savior. Now I receive angelic air force protection from all forms of evil desiring to take me out as my heart resides with Christ in Goshen – the Land of Drawing Near.

Above all, because we have a relationship with Jesus, our awareness will prevent us from taking the bait. We know what is demonic and what is Holy; therefore, our thinking will not become twisted because of the evil we encounter. When demonically inspired happenings attempt to sway us towards compromise, the coping mechanisms we will lean upon will be rooted in truthfulness rather than deceitfulness.

PRAYER

God Who Gives Us the Grace to Resist Evil,

Please reveal to us untrue thought patterns. Not only that Lord but help us cope with the stresses of law enforcement servanthood in ways that ensure evil will not overtake our mind. We acknowledge our need to function under Your strength to maintain biblical standards of integrity. Thank You!

PROMISE ELEVEN

Psalm 91:11-12

For He shall give His angels charge over you, To keep you in all your ways. In their hands they shall bear you up, Lest you dash your foot against a stone.

IF YOU WERE SATAN and were tasked with the self-generated assignment to bring to pass the destruction of the human species, what stone would you place in their path to make them trip, providing you an unfair advantage to eradicate them?

Surely, we understand Satan and his cohorts are behind the iniquitous propaganda that slowly chips at the foundations of Godly virtues like love, joy, peace, patience, goodness, kindness, gentleness, and self-control. The pursuit vehicle that follows close behind Satan's will for our lives is the tarnishing of God's character being diminished in the ambiance we find ourselves serving in.

Of course, we cannot rule out the stone tool that digs faith out of our heart and replaces it with hopelessness. It reminds me of a story. Satan was preparing for a garage sale when his apprentice began displaying some items for purchase. This little demonic helper offered Lucifer's most prized possession to a prospective buyer. This precious tool was Satan's favorite because he had used it and planned to continue to use this device to ensnare humankind throughout future ages. Quickly, Satan flew over to the little demon and shouted, "No! Do not put that out for sale. I have used this tool to trick many of God's children into blaming Him for their hardships rather than me. This is the wedge of discouragement, and without it I would lose influence over most of humanity."

Without a doubt, Satan's ploys center on controlling our minds, making us lose hope in God's promises. If left unchecked they lead to the first step that permits our flesh to control our inner person, rather than our spirit to control our body. What ensue are unprecedented amounts of despondency sometime leading to a preliminary step of suicide: the dreaded faith crisis.

Why write all this to teach how angels protect, lead, and minister to LEOs? The answer is two-fold. First, Satan tempted Jesus by offering Him an alternative plan than God's will, but the angels had already assisted in preparing Jesus for victory. Second, angels-built Jesus up after He was tempted which helped Him remain obedient to God's purpose for His life – fulfilling the role as the Lamb of God who takes away the sins of the world.

Matthew 4:1-11

Then Jesus was led up by the Spirit into the wilderness to be tempted by the devil. 2 And when He had fasted forty days and forty nights, afterward He was hungry. 3 Now when the tempter came to Him, he said, "If You are the Son of God, command that these stones become bread." 4 But He answered and said, "It is written, 'Man shall not live by bread alone, but by every word that proceeds from the mouth of God.'" 5 Then the devil took Him up into the holy city, set Him on the pinnacle of the temple, 6 and said to Him, "If You are the Son of God, throw Yourself down. For it is written:' He shall give His angels charge over you, 'and,' In their hands they shall bear you up, Lest you dash your foot against a stone.'" 7 Jesus said to him, "It is written again, 'You shall not tempt the Lord your God.'" 8 Again, the devil took Him up on an exceedingly high mountain, and showed Him all the kingdoms of the world and their glory. 9 And he said to Him, "All these things I will give You if You will fall down and worship me." 10 Then Jesus said to him, "Away with you, Satan! For it is written, 'You shall worship the Lord your God, and Him only you shall serve.'" 11 Then the devil left Him, and behold, angels came and ministered to Him. (End of Verse)

In reference, Satan committed the sin of presumption by hoping Jesus would abandon His reliance upon God, failing to fulfill the very purpose He was predestined to accomplish. Well, are you glad Jesus recognized Satan's trap and overcame his lies with the sword of the spirit, angelic support, and God's Word? I sure am!

Just as importantly and maybe even more so was how Satan implied to Jesus that God was holding out on Him. You see, when self-reliance connects with resentment it produces the elicit drug called PRIDE, I refer to it as the rock cocaine of the spiritual realm. This is usually indicative of attitudes that radiate in our conscience by saying things like, "This agency is holding out on me, they owe me because I have given my time, talents, and abilities to the cause."

Moreover, pride is the archenemy of gratefulness. This ego-infecting vector is relentless to convince that our heavenly gifts are self-generated. Sure, we must develop and maintain them, but without God's initial deposit within we would not have had any capital to work with in the first place! As it was for Satan and will be for all LEOs who allow pride to overtake them, one can take this to the bank: Pride goes before destruction and a haughty spirit before a fall. (Proverb 16:18) Many LEOs have dashed their foot against their unchecked ego who feels the need to protect itself in unhealthy pride. In my estimation, Sigmund Freud did a good job classifying the ego into the id, ego, and superego. Unfortunately, he had no spiritual solutions to offer on how to be set free from the imbalance they cause. His genius was on the correct path with the "talking cure" which did provide temporary relief for many of his patients' symptoms. However, he failed to discover how the prayer connection brings permanent healing, peace, and deliverance.

Truly, if we keep our focus on God rather than our self-generated pride, we can rest assured that if we are about to trip over a stone, God's angels will prevent us from falling. The stones may be literal or spiritual in nature, but regardless when we come across them, we can be sure they will not impede us from finishing the faith race of LEO servanthood.

Furthermore, experiences have taught that anytime I take on the assumption God is holding out on me, I stop the progression of His will for my life. This is extremely dangerous because His angels are more apt to protect when I follow His ways.

If I allow my attitude to reflect negatively towards God by being discouraged, it will hinder God's protection. It is extremely difficult for angels to help when I trust in myself rather than praying them into battle on my behalf. After all, who prays when they think they can handle difficulties without God's help? Answer: deceived religious people!

Worse yet is how pride twists our judgment between right and wrong and infects with the virus called self-righteousness. When we catch that self-centered infection, we are on our way to a premature demise. This judgmental disease will convince that every violation of law we encounter or investigate is a personal attack against us.

For example, I recall many instances when I had to step back from inmates who had disrespected the correctional officer authority delegated to me. Convicts can offend with their words in away that infuriate the ego to desire the escalation of a heated discussion rather than pour water on its flame. Luckily, the Holy Spirit always assisted me by providing the people skills to motivate inmates to comply without having to call in the Calvary.

There truly is power in the words we speak. Many of my former correctional officer counterparts can attest that the words spoken in a penitentiary have the power to bring order or a full-fledged riot into existence. It really does matter what we say and how we say it.

Moreover, foot and mouth disease are not only a LEO agriculture inspectors concern, but is symbolic of the many LEOs who have sabotaged their own career through decisive words.

The danger of thinking we are the law rather than stewards of the law, is the risk of overcompensating our delegated authority by stepping out from under our scope of employment. If that occurs, we will quickly learn that we only had authority because we were under authority.

Above all, our responsibility is to continue in faith-filled corresponding action to our calling. One way we do this is by throwing off any prideful attitudes we carry on our shoulders and replace them with the humility Jesus exhibited.

Jesus' willingness to depend on Psalm 91 is one preliminary decision that tipped the scales in His favor. It allowed victory over the temptation to circumvent God's plan of success for His future. Ask yourself this question: if it were incumbent upon Jesus to depend on God's angels in the face of adversity, why would we be exempt from doing the same?

PRAYER

God Who Dislikes Pride,

We trust in You rather than self-generated pride. As it says in Psalm 36:11-12 "Let not the foot of pride come against me, And let not the hand of the wicked drive me away." Our hope is in the promise that Your angels are commanded to protect and keep us in all Your ways. Help us walk in humility so we are not partakers with those who have tripped and unable to finish their race.

> James 1:6-8
>
> But let him ask in faith , with no doubting, for he who doubts is like a wave of the sea driven and tossed by the wind. 7 For let not that man suppose that he will receive anything from the Lord; 8 he is a double-minded man, unstable in all his ways.

PROMISE TWELVE

Psalm 91:13

You shall tread upon the lion and the cobra, the young lion and the serpent you shall trample underfoot.

WE HAVE A PROMISE FROM JESUS that the gates of Hell will not be able to stop us from bringing to pass righteousness on the earth. It was God's only begotten Son who said, "...On this rock I will build My church, and the gates of Hades shall not prevail against it. And I will give you the keys of the kingdom of heaven, and whatever you bind on earth will be bound in heaven, and whatever you loose on earth will be loosed in heaven." Matthew 16:18-19

Of course, that does not mean we are exempt from prohibiting Satan and his cohorts from having their way. Without LEOs upholding the societal system of order on the earth anarchy would take over. Even worse, the Christian church would be unable to do ministry works like teaching, preaching, and providing the awareness of God's healing power.

To illustrate, just imagine what it would be like if there was an announcement that a certain highway in the State you reside was not going to have any law enforcement responding to emergencies that occurred upon it; neither would LEOs be enforcing any of the laws of the land. Anarchy would ensue on a grand scale. Now, it is nice to know that as LEOs we are ordained to counterattack wickedness and prevail against its every form. We simply do this by participating in the LEO community by ensuring peaceful conditions exist within our areas of responsibility and authority. Freedom of choice creates conditions that permit the church liberty to preach the gospel.

Did you know that when Satan was quoting portions of Psalm 91 to Jesus, he conveniently did not mention the scripture prophesying his defeat? For sure, he is not stupid! The slippery serpent knew enough not to speak his own demise by reminding Jesus that God had promised Him ultimate victory over evil by trampling upon him. The point is, if Satan was wise enough to recognize the power of his words, why don't we? It was only a short time later that Jesus overcame Satan as it is described in Colossians 2:15: "Having disarmed principalities and powers, He *(Jesus)* made a public spectacle of them, triumphing over them in it. *(Emphasis mine).*

Even though Psalm 91:13 is referring to Jesus' infamous victory over the entities of darkness it still has major natural and spiritual significance for LEOs. God's protection is available as we come against legal violations rooted in selfish defiance towards the universal law of loving one's neighbor as one's self.

The lions that come against LEOs are those who have a stake in organized crime. These individuals may think they are getting away with violations towards the societal system of order; however, when LEO agencies and those who back up their authority within government say, "Enough is enough!" these self-deceived criminals begin to reap what they have sown. See: Romans Chapter 13: 1-7.

Unfortunately, history has proven that another species of the vicious cat family symbolic of Psalm 91 are corrupt politicians. These squeamish little predators, unctuous sycophants, have sold out their conscience for a few morsels of public exploitation. This can become discouraging for LEOs who become a casualty from the corruption that occurs between these separate but infiltrated groups. When this happens, LEOs can stand on the promise that the righteousness they represent and uphold will be victorious over all the lions that want to devour them. Know this: it does not matter how grown the lion is or how many are in the Pride, the truth is those led by integrity will trample upon them.

Let us be cognizant about serpents we navigate around in our career of law enforcement servanthood. These snakes in the grass are corrupt LEOs. You know, the ones that when you talk to them the pure evil abiding within must use all its restraint not to manifest itself outwardly. Thank God for internal affairs divisions, without them who knows how bad it would really be? Stand firm in knowing that even these serpents will not prevail against the LEO who is living up to the title he or she holds. Even if dirty officers try to undermine good police work, they will ultimately get their head squished just like corrupt politicians. The LEO Christian can rest assured the authority he or she represents will trample upon the heads of agency managers who desire to use their boa constrictor type fangs (unethical choices for career-preservation and advancement) to strike at the faithful LEO. It may seem impossible to overcome the size of these serpents, but rest assured that He (Holy Spirit) who is in the LEO Christian is much larger than Satan who is in the world. British evangelist, author, and faith healer of the early 20th century, Smith Wigglesworth, applied this truth and said, "I'm a thousand times bigger on the inside than I am on the outside." I like Smith's boldness because Satan needs reminding that we know whose authority our backup comes from.

Bible Patriarchs experienced the manifestation of the promises in Psalm 91 as they functioned under the power of the Holy Spirit. Moses used his authority to overcome the infestation of poisonous snakes. Sampson killed a lion with swiftness and ease. The underweight freckled shepherd boy, David, valiantly stood up to Goliath with only a slingshot and rock…bringing him down in one blow. Most likely, The Angel of the Lord's hand appeared just before the rock reached the giant's head, grabbed the stone, and powerfully smashed it into that uncircumcised Philistine's temple. He had defiled the armies of the living God for forty days, but when little David showed up in the Name of The Lord Almighty, off came the head of that blasphemer. See: 1 Samuel Chapter 17.

Of course, Daniel who was thrown into the lions' den was later pulled out without a scratch on his body. Then there was Paul, bitten by a venomous snake that did not affect him in the least. Moreover, the key to understanding our role regarding living in God's secret place of protection is to NOT go looking for grizzly bears and dangerous reptiles to test the validity of God's Word. What is important to know is when faced with adversity and danger doing what God has called us to – God is with us and fear is the opposite of faith. More important is understanding and practicing our authority 'In Christ'. The reason these giants of the faith were able to overcome their adversaries is the same reason Jesus was able to overcome Satan. They had a personal relationship with God, were obedient to His will, and had faith muscles so large they were able to knockout their opponents. To do likewise and become All-Stars of the Super Bowl of Faith, we must pattern after them.

It is one thing to test God by foolishly placing ourselves in dangerous situations, and another to encounter a crime in process ensuing from LEO vigilance. For example, if we go seeking dangerous situations just to get a rush of addictive adrenalin or prove how spiritual we are – we will not be functioning under the direction of the Holy Spirit and may end up like the 1920's Pentecostal preacher who started the rattlesnake-handling ministry, and ironically died from the venom one injected into him. Remember this: spirituality is rooted in maturity not stupidity!

Maybe you are asking, "Who represents the cobra in the jungle of law enforcement servanthood…that snake with the hood?" It is obvious to me, and most of us who serve in some arm of law enforcement that the venomous poison against the LEO community comes from many media outlets. Some of them spit malignant lies at LEO's under the protection of The First Amendment. These hypocrites will use freedom of speech as a defense to justify the destruction of LEOs and their families' lives. They do not stop with their satanically inspired agenda but are often caught concealing the truth they are called to proclaim. Is it any wonder that Pastor James wrote: "Even so the tongue is a little member and boasts great things. See how great a forest a little fire kindles! And the tongue is a fire, a world of iniquity. The tongue is so set among our members that it defiles the whole body and sets on fire the course of nature, and it is set on fire by hell. For every kind of beast and bird, of reptile and creature of the sea, is tamed and has been tamed by mankind. But no man can tame the tongue. It is an unruly evil, full of deadly poison**."** James 3:5-8

Therefore, when you see that van with the cobra hood (satellite dish) upon its roof, I recommend you follow the Wisdom of Solomon:

(Proverb 29:11)

A fool vents all his feelings, but a wise man holds them back.

(Proverbs 17:28)

Even a fool is counted wise when he holds his peace; when he shuts his lips, he is considered perceptive.

With Psalm 91:13 in our corner and wisdom to handle dangers we encounter, there is no doubt we will be victorious in eradicating them from our agencies, communities, and nations.

PRAYER

God Who We Hope In,

We uphold our confession of faith that we are victorious over Satan's works and those who desire to bring his agenda to fruition. Our hope is in the promises in Your Word. Give us the fortitude needed to stand in the victory You have provided. Teach us to walk in Your power to overcome natural threats, spiritual lions, and media serpents. Thank You!

1 John 5:4-5
For whatever is born of God overcomes the world. And this is the victory that has overcome the world — our faith . Who is he who overcomes the world, but he who believes that Jesus is the Son of God?

PROMISE THIRTEEN

Psalm 91:14

Because he has set his love upon Me, therefore I will deliver him; I will set him on high, because he has known My name.

IT IS NOT ABOUT RELIGION my precious brothers and sisters in law enforcement. God is not concerned with ritual and tradition as many have told you. As the author of the controversial book, 'The Deception of Religion' wrote: "One aspect of religious deception is the belief that people attain God's standard of righteousness by engaging in ritualistic pious observances."

What is God concerned about? Answer: He wants us to grow into a personal relationship with Him, Jesus, and the Holy Spirit. This will free us from bondage and deliver us from evil. Deliverance is a preliminary step in helping others experience God's grace.

When we truly know His Name the protection available through Psalm 91 will have entry into our lives. God wants us to benefit from this mystery so eternity with Him is a partnership rather than a dictatorship. It really is that simple!

Look at the above verse. What does it say is the prerequisite for God to deliver us? It says: if we set our love upon Him. IF — gives the option to choose to follow God or go our own way and try to make it work without Him. For me, I attempted that the first twenty-three years of my life and it only worsened. God — the universal intelligence who is the one in three and three in one of the Holy Trinity is implying that when we know His Name, we have entered a contract with Him. God's part of the agreement is to deliver us from trouble and set us on high.

In the same light, our part of the covenant is to live out his assignments, for His will, that he has commissioned us to do. These include our heartfelt sacrifices to advance the gospel message and remain intimate with the Name of Jesus.

To expound, knowing His Name means to be cognizant of what His Name represents, to know who He is, to know the prophecies He has fulfilled, to know what He accomplished by going to the Cross of Calvary, to know His passions by spending intimate time with Him. To know is much more than believing Jesus exists. The Devil believes, but he is not a beneficiary of Psalm 91. However, us who have taken the time to discover how great, how loving, and how forgiving God is – we know His Name.

Just think about this for a moment. God is promising that our relationship with Him will determine the level of divine intervention in our lives. This truth is clear to me and I am confident confirms witness with you. We must remind ourselves there is a requirement to build our friendship with God just as we do in the natural with other LEO's, our children, significant other, and acquaintances. However, the benefits obtained from knowing the character of God far outweigh the amount of time we invest in prayer and fellowship with Him. We will not only come out on top in the adversities we face as LEOs, but the tribulations that come our way will be what God will use to transcend us to the highest levels within our agencies. God has a knack for taking the unfortunate happenings in our careers and turning them into monuments that defy the very forces that came against us. As the old cliché say's, "If life gives you lemons, make lemonade!" This is not hard for Jesus to do because He turned water into wine. Living 'In Christ', provides the ability to transform into His likeness.

Many people do not know that the Name Jesus Christ has more power than the Name Jesus of Nazareth. They ask, how? I usually tell them that Jesus received the Name above all names: 'Jesus the Christ', after He resurrected from the dead, defeated Satan in battle, and took His rightful seat at God's right hand.

For example, in Colossians 2:15, it states: "Having disarmed principalities and powers, He made a public spectacle of them, triumphing over them in it." This alludes to the way defeated enemies were humiliated during ancient times.

To illustrate, the common practice in antiquity warfare was the winning general would strip the king of the defeated territory down to his under garments, put him in stocks and bonds, more understood in this modern age as leg-irons and handcuffs. Next, he would proceed to parade the defeated foe throughout the conquered lands in a humiliated and degraded manner. This sent a clear message to all the inhabitants of that region that the king who was a ruler was now equivalent to a slave.

With that said, after Jesus rose from the dead, he removed the demonic entities blocking the pathway from earth to heaven. The reason Jesus had so much power to overcome Satan and his armies is because obedience to God's will strengthened Him spiritually to overcome disobedient Satan. Consequently, the authority Satan had over souls is no longer legal when they trust in the promise recorded John 14:6: Jesus said to him, "I am the way, the truth, and the life. No one comes to the Father except through Me.

On another note, it appears to me that Psalm 91:1-13 are referring to how Jesus would overcome the perilous times during His life on earth. It is in verse 14 I recognize that Jesus is acknowledged as speaking to the church because God rewarded Him for His obedience and actually called Jesus God in Hebrews 1:8-9: But to the Son He says: "Your throne, O God, is forever and ever; A scepter of righteousness is the scepter of Your kingdom. You have loved righteousness and hated lawlessness; Therefore God, Your God, has anointed You with the oil of gladness more than Your companions." I find it extremely exciting that the promise God gave to Jesus became ours after He resurrected from the dead. However, many, if not all biblical scholars disagree with me on this inference that Jesus is also speaking the last three scriptures in Psalm 91; but, I still think Jesus is talking to the church and God is speaking to Jesus. Wow! Jesus who was the subject of the entire Psalm takes the place of God on our behalf making us partakers with Him. Jesus then proceeds to promise us deliverance and the same benefits God had sworn to provide Him on earth.

Therefore, every LEO Christian can make claim to the promises spoken by God to Jesus within this prophetic utterance. You see, Jesus is our God…He is our representative and protector from all the dangers spoken of in this Psalm. Do not take my word at face value without biblical backup, but read what Jesus said recorded in John 10:27-30, "My sheep hear My voice, and I know them, and they follow Me. And I give them eternal life, and they shall never perish; neither shall anyone snatch them out of My hand. My Father, who has given them to Me, is greater than all; and no one is able to snatch them out of My Father's hand. I and My Father are one." As we study Jesus' character we grow into a deeper relationship with the Holy Trinity.

Likewise, it is extremely difficult to remain outside of God's will when we study the Word of God and allow the Spirit of Christ to influence our thinking. Once our thinking has been renewed to the truth found in God's Word – nothing will be able to prevail against us.

PRAYER

God Who is Jesus,

Our desire is to grow in relationships with You, Jesus, and the Holy Spirit. Assist in making our fellowship with the Holy Trinity the focus of our personal and professional lives. It is through the awareness of Your true character that deliverance from evil will manifest in our lives. Thank You!

PROMISE FOURTEEN

Psalm 91:15

He shall call upon Me, and I will answer him; I will be with him in trouble; I will deliver him and honor him.

LOOK AT WHAT JESUS SAYS HE WILL DO. He will answer and be with us in trouble as He simultaneously delivers and honors us. Now, why would He say those things if they were not true? Does God the Father, Jesus, and the Holy Spirit have any reason at all to lie?

Absolutely not! If they prevaricated, Holiness would depart from them. This would require them to forfeit their role as Deity. We can rest assured that if they said it – it is surer than low temperatures, snow, and ice in my rural hometown Batavia, New York, during January.

One preliminary action necessary to receive the benefits promised in Psalm 91 is to humble our pride and call upon God. Why do so many LEOs refuse to ask the Lord to help them? Is it because they are afraid He will intervene and by doing so provide credence to the truth of His Word?

Knowing that God is real and will hold humankind accountable for their behavior, sometimes hinders people from accepting the bible as truth. This attitude of rejection contributes to many remaining in their sinful bondages rather than deciding to accept and apply the knowledge necessary to step out of darkness and walk towards Christ's glorious light.

I am not judging them; however, my estimation is they are afraid of being accountable to truth requiring responsibility on their part to change their non-heavenly behaviors.

Do you know why sometimes it seems to take a little while to get our prayers answered? After all, He does say, "I will answer him." When God answers, we grow to know His character. Most people do not know that the First Epistle of John Chapter 5:14-15, teaches: "Now this is the confidence that we have in Him, that if we ask anything according to His will, He hears us. And if we know that He hears us, whatever we ask, we know that we have the petitions that we have asked of Him." Sometimes God's spiritual email does not show up in our inbox until a few miles down the road. Maybe, it will be a day, week, or even a year or more before it pops up. Regardless, as far as God is concerned, He clicked the send icon immediately. One thing taught during the time we wait for answers to our prayers is faith in the sovereignty God has over our lives. You see, time came out of God; therefore, it will always do what God pleases. Since God created time it would be against the natural order of things for this infinite intelligence to be in submission to it. This is why we need to be proactive in our prayer lives regarding not only daily needs, but for angelic protection to show up if we come face to face with an assailant that intends to cause us a premature demise. With Psalm 91 intricately woven in us, nothing will be able to overtake us, especially when we are listening to the Holy Spirit that abides within us.

Unlike some Christian denominations, I believe Romans 10:13 that says, "Whoever calls on the name of the Lord shall be saved." Are you a Whoever? I am, and I invite you to call on the Name of the Lord as I did. Maybe you are saying to yourself, "Yeah, but you don't know what I have done." Guess what – I do not care and neither does God. Jesus took care of that and now it is up to you to either receive His forgiveness or reject it. Just as the old cliché goes: the ball is in your court. Please accept the gift of God – His Son – as your Savior and friend.

Maybe you have heard the saying: prosecution is not persecution. I find it interesting when Christians believe the consequences of a bad decision are the fault of Satan and/or someone other than themselves. It seems the truths surrounding the universal law of cause and effect have eluded them. Therefore, the lie they are victims of the whims of chance creates a stronghold in their mind. The Devil made me do it is a ridiculous excuse!

Our experiences as LEOs have taught that people who repeatedly fail to take responsibility for their lives are their own worst enemies. Now let us be truthful and answer this question: "What problems have we brought upon ourselves due to poor attitudes related to our LEO roles?" You know, the troubles we deal with in our agencies including conflicts with management and contemporaries. These hindrances are sometimes traceable to our twisted perceptions and failure to accept our rank in the paramilitary structure. I have learned that when my authority on a matter is exhausted, my responsibility regarding it has sufficed. Too often, we respond to the decisions made within our agencies as personal attacks against us. When they are choices made by those chosen to stand in that office. Upper management may have promoted them based on their ability to see the bigger picture regarding the needs of their agency. Unfortunately, some of them lack necessary people skills and reprimand the entire police force when an officer makes a mistake, showing a lack of leadership on their part. Rather than calling that individual on the carpet, they put a bullet in the morale of the troops by harping on the negatives. As a seasoned LEO stated, "If someone (*%#%@) their pants they give toilet-paper to everybody." (Intimation implied) I agree, sometimes that statement hits the nail right on the head. However, in all fairness to management, we should consider the possibility they are wisely using the mishap as an opportunity to warn officers regarding the dangers of being complacent. They use this technique as they simultaneously render mercy towards an officer who unintentionally messed all over him or herself. Law enforcement supervisors have a difficult job, I know – I use to be one. Show mercy to them and they just may pay it forward even if they received their rank because of their membership in the Three F Club: Friends, Family, and Favorites. Know this: setting everyone within our agencies straight is not our calling. We may believe that it is, but this comes from our hubris that says we are empowered to do something we are not. Allowing the system of protocol to function without rebelling against it keeps us under its protection. However, if we foment over every little change of procedure by bucking against them and sowing discontent within our agencies, God may just allow us to reap the poisonous harvest we have planted.

Why? Because we have apparently attempted to bring change through our flesh rather than by trusting God to answer our prayers – that is if we bothered to pray in the first place. Are you glad God is merciful? I sure am! He will help even when we do not deserve it. He really cares about us. He loves us more than words can express. The problem is if we fail to spend ample time in prayer and fellowship with Him, we are more susceptible to believe the lie that we cannot come to Him in our obvious time of need. Since we must first ask to receive…we do not receive because we fail to ask. When we proceed to walk in faith by calling upon His Name, He will be with us in trouble. Not only that but Jesus' diaphanous light will be manifested through us. The exciting thing about this truth is we will receive honor in this current age and those dispensations lurking in the shadows of elsewhere.

PRAYER

God Who Tells Us to Call on Him,

Today we set all our preconceived solutions to the problems of the world aside and make a conscientious decision to CALL ON YOU. It is obvious our attempts to change things without first praying and asking for Your help only makes them worse. Help us to understand that if we want to receive Your protection, deliverance, and honor – we must first invite You into our lives. Thank You!

PROMISE FIFTEEN

Psalm 91:16

With long life I will satisfy him, And show him My salvation.

I HAVE SAID THE FOLLOWING FROM THE TIME I entered law enforcement as a State Correctional Officer in 1994, and I will continue to confess it for the rest of my natural life. It may sometimes make me come across overconfident, but I realize the need to decide before hand that I will finish the race God has enlisted me in and live many years. Moreover, I will overcome all threats from inmates, criminal suspects, disease, and accidents related to my law enforcement assignments. For sure, I will not report to heaven until I am ready. It takes faith to speak this because what if something occurs and I lose my life in the line of duty? Will it make the promises in God's Word and especially Psalm 91 untrue? Answer: Of course not!

God enjoys using us to validate His Word, but He can also prove its veracity without our help. REMEMBER THIS: it always falls on humanity if it appears His Word is contrary to what we witnessed or experienced in the natural. This truth applies to us as LEOs and in our personal lives. Rest assured that if we wait long enough, the truth of why bad things happened would prove that it is never God's fault. There is excessive blame gaming going on in law enforcement agencies. I once heard someone say, "It use to be, its not if you win or lose that matters, but how you play the game. But that has been changed to, it is not if you win or lose that matters but how you place the blame." Some LEOs believe God is using their agency mangers as channels to sabotage their career.

As biblical history proves – if God were out to get them, they would already be ashes! It is time for us to take God at His Word, rebuke fear, and trust what He has said. Let us keep it real and admit we either believe Him or we do not. Even more so – we are either trusting that Jesus was resurrected from the dead or living a lie that we are OK without Him.

Knowing that Jesus Christ is our Lord and Savior and applying that to our lives ensures victory as we proceed in faith. When we have fulfilled His purpose for our life, only then will we be truly satisfied. To stand means to stake our ground as we discussed in the teaching on Psalm 91:1, by putting Him first in our lives and casting off the sins that prevent us from obeying His Word.

Maybe you are asking, "What about all the LEOs who have known Jesus as their Savior, but died in the line of duty…doesn't their deaths prove Psalm 91 is not true?" I say, "Surely, that is a valid question and the answer has many ramifications; but have you considered the individuals responsibility to God regarding the promises in Psalm 91? How can we truly know if the law officer who gave his or her life for the societal system of order ever understood or applied these promises to his or her life? We simply do not know, but we can agree with the writer of Hebrews that by two immutable things, in which it is impossible for God to lie, we might have strong consolation, who have fled for refuge to lay hold of the hope set before us." See: Hebrews 6:18

The hope set before us is truly knowing Christ. 1 John 2:3-6 says, "Now by this we know that we know Him, if we keep His commandments. He who says, "I know Him," and does not keep His commandments, is a liar, and the truth is not in him. But whoever keeps His word, truly the love of God is perfected in him. By this we know that we are in Him. He who says he abides in Him ought himself also to walk just as He walked." When we walk fearlessly, obediently, and faithfully in Christ's Spirit - Psalm 91 will come through for us as it did for Jesus. After all, this book has over 23,000 words accredited to it and has only touched the surface of the promises behind these scriptures. Furthermore, the hope set before us comes from trusting in Jesus to guide our steps. When we listen to His Voice, the innate spiritual leading within our conscious; the all knowing Spirit that warns of danger, the infinite intelligence who gives a check in our Spirit to take an alternate route; then we are qualified to demand angelic protection and have become beneficiaries of Psalm 91 and 1 John 2:27, "But the anointing which you have received from Him abides in you, and you do not need that anyone teach you; but as the same anointing teaches you concerning all things, and is true, and is not a lie, and just as it has taught you, you will abide in Him." Regardless of the adversities we encounter, our intimate relationship with God will ensure natural and spiritual victory. The power of God works within and through teaching how to be victorious. We entered the right to divine protection and eternal life the moment we accepted Christ as Lord and Savior. The Bible calls us: 'In Christ', Born-Again, The Apple of God's Eye, and 'He Who Dwells in the Secret Place of the Most High'.

Moreover, God has promised that we can live a long and satisfied life. Understanding that a person can live a life of 100 years in a 50-year span, and another can live a life of 50 years in a 100-year span, is essential to interpreting Psalm 91:16. The quality, purpose, and impact of a life determine its spiritual longevity – not its biological age. Likewise, fulfilling the will of God is the secret to the meaning of life.

When God is pleased with what a person has done with his or her days on earth, they will know a satisfaction that the world cannot provide. Understanding the differences between spiritual and biological ages assists in understanding how God views how long a person has lived.

Furthermore, few have honestly found the greater contentment through dying for a virtuous cause, and the freedom of becoming truthful to one's self. Those who have decided and have been given the opportunities to stand for the preservation of conscience, the principle of unified egalitarianism, and/or the freedom of the soul – human liberty; have surely crossed over experiencing the satisfaction of laying down their life and freedom in order to shed light on the path leading to God. These luminaries like Confucius, Socrates, Abraham Lincoln, Gandhi, the Martyred Saints, and JESUS OF NAZARETH are only a small fraction representing the personal sacrifice of many who decided to develop altruism so others may know truth.

Obviously, a satisfied life is the peaceful reassurance that one's actions of sacrificial love make the world a better place for future generations. Without a doubt, the discovery of why God has left us imprisoned in our earth-suit after we have received Jesus as our Savior, will be revealed as we spend time in the Secret Place. When an individual who seeks and then finds their Heaven decreed assignment, he or she can then choose obedience or rebellion. Obedience is the nutrition for a life of spiritual growth; whereas rebellion is a cancer that resists Heaven's call resulting in an eternity of regret. To die at a young age for a great cause, is to live an impacting life of satisfaction as one enters an existence of eternal fulfillment. For those who have transcended above their flesh, their ego, and their pre-Christ spirit – they have passed many mile markers on the road leading to Heaven.

In contrast, those who have not traveled many miles upon that route still need angelic intervention, continued spiritual growth, and wisdom lessons as they develop in their godlike maturation. The world changers who have come before us for the betterment of humanity – regardless of their biological ages at physical death – have lived long knowledgeable lives, taught us how to redeem lost time, stepped out of their bodies, graduated unto higher enlightenment and heard God say, "Well done my good and faithful servant." I have not fulfilled all of God's will for my life as I seek the gap to fill; therefore, I still need to make a claim upon Psalm 91:16. When my test arrives as it did for the beacons of light that have come before me; I hope that God's righteousness will radiate light from my spirit-man unto the path Jesus traveled, that led Him to Golgotha's Hill.

PRAYER

God Who Shows Us Your Salvation,

You showed Your salvation when Jesus hung on the cross for our sins. It is through what He did that allows us to know You and have eternal life. As Your Word promises in Romans 10:9-13, "that if you confess with your mouth the Lord Jesus and believe in your heart that God has raised Him from the dead, you will be saved. For with the heart one believes unto righteousness, and with the mouth confession is made unto salvation. For the Scripture says, "Whoever believes on Him will not be put to shame." For there is no distinction between Jew and Greek, for the same Lord over all is rich to all who call upon Him. "For whoever calls on the name of the Lord shall be saved." Thereupon, we confess He is our Lord and believe in our heart that You raised Him from the dead. Above all, we stand in faith knowing that when we cross over into the next realm of existence, we will surely see our salvation (Jesus). Thank You!

> **1 Peter 1:22-23**
>
> Since you have purified your souls in obeying the truth through the Spirit in sincere love of the brethren, love one another fervently with a pure heart, 23 having been born again, not of corruptible seed but incorruptible, through the word of God which lives and abides forever...

> **UNIFIED PRAYER OF PROTECTION FOR LAW OFFICERS**

God of Psalm 91,

As Jesus dwells at Your right side we know He is making intercession for LEOs. He is our Great High Priest who sympathizes with all our weaknesses; and for this reason, we stand in faith knowing the Holy Trinity is protecting and watching out for our best interests. Above all, we proclaim that You are the refuge and fortress that protects. Because we know You, Jesus, and the Holy Spirit, there is power available that strengthens us to overcome every struggle.

We commit to spend more time in Your Holy presence beholding Your beauty each day. We know that when we are in trouble You are with us. We will continue to rejoice by praising You all the days of our lives and forever more. As a result, times of turmoil and stress will affect us like water upon a duck's back. With that said, we are victorious in everything we put our hands to, and our efforts are blessed by You.

We proclaim: the demon forces that came against Jesus were completely defeated by Him, and we are victorious against all who come against us because of our relationship with You. Above all, we rebuke all sickness and disease. With the promises in Your Word, along with our relationship with the Great High Priest Jesus and the Holy Spirit – we have no reason to fear. We give praise to Your Name for hearing when we pray and allowing entrance into the Holy of Holies to have fellowship with You.

Oh Lord, we need Your help in a grand way. Law enforcement officers are committing suicide at alarming rates; however, it seems that too few are responding to the call of this epidemic.

Please move upon the management and leadership of every law enforcement agency on earth to implement suicide prevention and emotional survival training to their officers. As You know Lord, law enforcement officers are committing suicide at two times the rate of line of duty deaths. This should grieve the hearts of those that have authority in their agencies to make significant changes that benefit their officers. It saddens us when they continue to treat officers worse than cattle by being completely insensitive to their needs, and the ramifications hyper-vigilance has on their personal and professional lives. We are grateful because You hear and respond when we pray.

We guard our peace by prohibiting Satan and His cohorts from stealing it. You have provided hope that passes all understanding and we refuse to doubt Your goodness. Assist in controlling our minds, wills, and emotions – for we know Satan comes against us through our thinking to paralyze with fear.

Moreover, he shoots false perceptions our way trying to convince that Your Word cannot protect from sickness and disease. Because of this we wear, our spiritual prayer vest to stop lies he shoots that can cause internal injuries to our faith.

Just as You protected the baby Jesus from the murderous agenda of king Herod, we know that when we are out numbered and about to be defeated in battle You will warn, protect, and lead us to safety. Likewise, as multitudes of police officers become suicidal statistics, our relationship with You will ensure we will not be one of them.

We are thankful for all the Holy Spirit has and continues to do for us. He has made it perfectly clear in Psalm 91 that we will not suffer the consequences of the wicked.

Continually remind us that we are victorious when contending against anarchy. Above all, our conquering spirit will assist in bringing to pass the fruits of their unrighteous folly. Remind us that when it appears evildoers are prospering – we know they will eventually reap what they have sown.

We desire to grow into a personal relationship with You, Jesus, and the Holy Spirit. It is through this type of intimacy that surrounds us by Your grace and protection. Furthermore, help us recognize any areas of our lives that are hindering our friendship with You. Assist us in tapping into the power available to overcome all idols.

Please reveal to us untrue thought patterns. Not only that Lord but help us cope with the stresses of law enforcement servanthood in ways that ensure evil will not overtake us. We really do acknowledge our need to function under Your strength to maintain biblical standards of integrity.

We trust in You rather than self-generated pride. As it says in Psalm 36:11-12…" Let not the foot of pride come against me, And let not the hand of the wicked drive me away." Our hope is in the promise that Your angels are commanded to protect and keep us in all Your ways. Help us walk in humility so we are not partakers with those who have tripped and unable to finish their race.

We uphold our confession of faith that we are victorious over Satan's works and those who desire to bring his agenda to fruition. Our hope is in the promises in Your Word. Give us the fortitude needed to stand in the victory You have provided. Teach us to walk in Your power to overcome natural threats, spiritual lions, and media serpents. Our desire is to grow in relationships with You, Jesus, and the Holy Spirit. Assist in making our fellowship with the Holy Trinity the focus of our personal and professional lives. It is through the awareness of Your true character that deliverance from evil will manifest in our lives.

Today we set all our preconceived solutions to the problems of the world aside and make a conscientious decision to CALL ON YOU. It is obvious our attempts to change things without first praying and asking for Your help only makes them worse. Help us to understand that if we want to receive Your protection, deliverance, and honor – we must first invite You into our lives.

You showed Your salvation when Jesus hung on the cross for our sins. It is through what He did that allows us to know You and have eternal life. As Your Word promises in Romans 10:9-13, "that if you confess with your mouth the Lord Jesus and believe in your heart that God has raised Him from the dead, you will be saved. For with the heart one believes unto righteousness, and with the mouth confession is made unto salvation. For the Scripture says, "Whoever believes on Him will not be put to shame." For there is no distinction between Jew and Greek, for the same Lord over all is rich to all who call upon Him. "For whoever calls on the name of the Lord shall be saved."

Thereupon, we confess He is our Lord and believe in our heart You raised Him from the dead. Above all, we stand in faith knowing that when we cross over into the next realm of existence, we will surely see our salvation (Jesus). Thank You!

ABOUT THE AUTHOR

David P. Wlazlak received ministerial ordination in 2008 and has encouraged others through his inspirational writings since 2007, his vast scope of audiences has reached across many venues and into the hearts and minds of those within spiritual and law enforcement communities. David's life purpose is to raise Christ Consciousness by assisting others in discovering who they are In-Christ. David is a prolific author, Bible School graduate, public-speaker, and chaplain who has ministered in various leadership roles, in both the private and public sectors. David's unique literary works are available on various platforms and include:

The Watchman's Plea

The Deception of Religion

Spiritual Insights for Law Officers

The Psalm 91 Project: Heavenly Backup for Law Enforcement

The 365 Day Law Enforcement Officer Devotional

The Ministry of Law Enforcement

Backwards BOBO: The Case of the Missing Dinosaur Nose (Coauthored)

My Little Book of I AM Affirmations /Christian & General Edition
The ABC's of Positivity

The Leader's Guide of I AM Affirmations
The ABC's of Positivity for Developing Team Members

The Pastor's Guide of I AM Affirmations
The ABC's of Positivity for Developing Parishioners

The Teacher's Guide of I AM Affirmations
The ABC's of Positivity for Developing Scholars

The Parent's Guide of I AM Affirmations
The ABC's of Positive Sayings for Sons

The Parent's Guide of I AM Affirmations
The ABC's of Positive Sayings for Daughters

The Husband's Guide of I AM Affirmations
The ABC's of Positive Sayings for Wives

The Wife's Guide of I AM Affirmations
The ABC's of Positive Sayings for Husbands

The Grandparent's Guide of I AM Affirmations
The ABC's of Positive Sayings for Grandchildren

I AM Affirmations for Law Enforcement Officers
The ABC's of Positivity for Developing LEO Character

The Life Partner's Guide of I Am Affirmations
The ABC's of Positive Sayings for Life Partners

The I AM Anthology /The ABC's of Positive Sayings for Humanity
Compilation of the Twelve I AM Guides

The I AM Family Edition
The ABC's of Positive Sayings for Families

Morning Noon & Nighttime Prayers for Families
Compilation of the Sixteen Family Devotionals

Morning Noon & Nighttime Prayers for Spiritual Enhancement
An Individual's One Hundred Heartfelt Proclamations

Morning Noon & Nighttime Family Prayers
One Hundred Heartfelt Proclamations for Our Family

Morning Noon & Nighttime Prayers for My Husband
A Wife's One Hundred Heartfelt Proclamations

Morning Noon & Nighttime Prayers for My Wife
A Husband's One Hundred Heartfelt Proclamations

Morning Noon & Nighttime Prayers for My Son
A Parent's One Hundred Heartfelt Proclamations

Morning Noon & Nighttime Prayers for My Daughter
A Parent's One Hundred Heartfelt Proclamations

Morning Noon & Nighttime Prayers for My Father
One Hundred Heartfelt Proclamations for Dad

Morning Noon & Nighttime Prayers for My Mother
One Hundred Heartfelt Proclamations for Mom

Morning Noon & Nighttime Prayers for My Grandfather
One Hundred Heartfelt Proclamations for Granddad

Morning Noon & Nighttime Prayers for My Grandmother
One Hundred Heartfelt Proclamations for Grandma

Morning Noon & Nighttime Prayers for My Grandson
A Grandparent's One Hundred Heartfelt Proclamations

Morning Noon & Nighttime Prayers for My Granddaughter
A Grandparent's One Hundred Heartfelt Proclamations

Morning Noon & Nighttime Prayers for My Brother
A Sibling's One Hundred Heartfelt Proclamations

Morning Noon & Nighttime Prayers for My Sister
A Sibling's One Hundred Heartfelt Proclamations

Morning Noon & Nighttime Prayers for My Uncle
One Hundred Heartfelt Proclamations for Uncles

Morning Noon & Nighttime Prayers for My Aunt
One Hundred Heartfelt Proclamations for Aunts

Morning Noon & Nighttime Prayers for My Nephew
One Hundred Heartfelt Proclamations for Nephews

Morning Noon & Nighttime Prayers for My Niece
One Hundred Heartfelt Proclamations for Nieces

One Hundred Prayerful Poems and Affirmations for Church Unity
A Chaplain's Heartfelt Proclamations to Guide the Body of Christ into One Accord

https://amazon.com/author/davidwlazlak

www.ingramcontent.com/pod-product-compliance
Lightning Source LLC
Chambersburg PA
CBHW051537240526
45465CB00027B/602